Peadar O'Donnell

THE IRISH WRITERS SERIES

James F. Carens, General Editor

TITLE	*AUTHOR*
SEAN O'CASEY	Bernard Benstock
J. C. MANGAN	James Kilroy
W. R. RODGERS	Darcy O'Brien
STANDISH O'GRADY	Phillip L. Marcus
PAUL VINCENT CARROLL	Paul A. Doyle
SEUMAS O'KELLY	George Brandon Saul
SHERIDAN LEFANU	Michael Begnal
AUSTIN CLARKE	John Jordan
BRIAN FRIEL	D. E. S. Maxwell
DANIEL CORKERY	George Brandon Saul
EIMAR O'DUFFY	Robert Hogan
MERVYN WALL	Robert Hogan
FRANK O'CONNOR	James Matthews
JOHN BUTLER YEATS	Douglas Archibald
LORD EDWARD DUNSANY	Zack Bowen
MARIA EDGEWORTH	James Newcomer
MARY LAVIN	Zack Bowen
OSCAR WILDE	Edward Partridge
SOMERVILLE AND ROSS	John Cronin
SUSAN L. MITCHELL	Richard M. Kain
J. M. SYNGE	Robin Skelton
KATHARINE TYNAN	Marilyn Gaddis Rose
LIAM O'FLAHERTY	James O'Brien
IRIS MURDOCH	Donna Gerstenberger
JAMES STEPHENS	Birgit Bramsbäck
BENEDICT KIELY	Daniel Casey
EDWARD MARTYN	Robert Christopher
DOUGLAS HYDE	Gareth Dunleavy
EDNA O'BRIEN	Grace Eckley
CHARLES LEVER	M. E. Elliott
BRIAN MOORE	Jeanne Flood
SAMUEL BECKETT	Clive Hart
ELIZABETH BOWEN	Edwin J. Kenney
JOHN MONTAGUE	Frank Kersnowski
ROBERT MATURIN	Robert E. Lougy
GEORGE FITZMAURICE	Arthur E. McGuinness

MICHAEL MCCLAVERTY	Leo F. McNamara
FRANCIS STUART	J. H. Natterstad
PATRICK KAVANAGH	Darcy O'Brien
BRINSLEY MACNAMARA	Raymond J. Porter
AND GEORGE SHIELS	
JACK B. YEATS	Robin Skelton
WILLIAM ALLINGHAM	Alan Warner
SAMUEL LOVER	Mabel Worthington
FLANN O'BRIEN	Bernard Benstock
DENIS JOHNSTON	James F. Carens
WILLIAM LARMINIE	Richard J. Finneran
SIR SAMUEL FERGUSON	Malcolm Brown
LADY GREGORY	Hazard Adams
GEORGE RUSSELL (AE)	Richard M. Kain and
	James O'Brien
DION BOUCICAULT	Peter A. Tasch
THOMAS DAVIS	Eileen Ibarra
LOUIS MACNEICE	Christopher Armitage
PADRAIC COLUM	Charles Burgess
PEADAR O'DONNELL	Grattan Freyer
OLIVER ST. JOHN GOGARTY	J. B. Lyons
THOMAS KINSELLA	David Clark
SEAN O'FAOLAIN	Joseph Browne
F. R. HIGGINS	Timothy Brownlow

PEADAR O'DONNELL

Grattan Freyer

Lewisburg
BUCKNELL UNIVERSITY PRESS

© 1973 by Associated University Presses, Inc.

Associated University Presses, Inc.
Cranbury, New Jersey 08512

Library of Congress Cataloging in Publication Data

Freyer, Grattan.
    Peadar O'Donnell.

    (The Irish writers series)
    Bibliography: p.
    1. O'Donnell, Peadar.
PR6029.D53Z66   823'.9'12   73-487
ISBN 0-8387-1362-9
ISBN 0-8387-1369-6 (pbk.)

Printed in the United States of America

Contents

Chronology

1893: born February 22 on small farm at Meenmore, near Dungloe, County Donegal. Fifth of nine children.

1911: entered teachers' training college in Drumcondra.

1913: returned to Donegal; assistant teacher at Innisfree; at Deryhenny; then principal teacher on Aranmore; begins to practice writing.
visited Scotland, meeting trade-unionist and socialist agitators.

1918: became full-time organizer for Irish Transport and General Workers' Union in northeastern counties.

1919: joined Volunteers, which soon became the Irish Republican Army; guerilla war developing in Ireland.

1920: resigned from ITGWU to serve fulltime in IRA.

May 1921: wounded in action against British.

July 1921: cease-fire; Anglo-Irish Treaty proposals cause split in IRA; O'Donnell takes anti-Treaty side; with rank of Commandant-General on Republican Army Executive.

July 1922: captured on fall of the Four Courts in Dublin by Free State forces; in various Irish jails.

March 16, 1924: escaped from Curragh camp.

June 25, 1924: married Lile O'Donel in Dublin.

1924–26: editor of *An t'Oglach,* illegal organ of IRA.

1925–32: agitation over Land Annuities.

1926–34: editor of *An Phoblacht.*

1925 or '26: published *Storm.*

1927: *Islanders.*

1928: visited USA.

1929: *Adrigoole.*

1930: *The Knife.*

1932: *The Gates Flew Open.*
Wrack produced for one week at Abbey Theatre, Dublin; revived for one week, 1935.

1932–36: living in Achill.

1934: *On the Edge of the Stream.*
With George Gilmore and Frank Ryan broke away from IRA to form Republican Congress. editor of *Republican Congress.*

1936: holidaying in Spain when Spanish civil war begins; returns to Ireland; organizing support for Spanish Republic; published *Salud!*

1939: second visit to USA—six months' social visit; in Dublin on outbreak of World War II.

1940: *The Bell* (monthly periodical) founded by Sean O'Faolain with O'Donnell's active help.

1940–43: temporary welfare officer with Irish Department of Social Welfare; visited wartime England and Scotland.

April 1946: succeeded O'Faolain as editor of *The Bell.*

1948: refused visa to visit USA.
1953: visited Poland and Hungary: delegate to World Peace Congress.
1954: *The Bell* ceased publication.
 The Big Windows.
1958–64: Hon. Secretary to Irish Academy of Letters.
1963: published *There Will be Another Day.*
1965: with Dan Breen founded Irish Voice on Vietnam.
1969: Lile O'Donnell died; buried at Foxford, County Mayo.

Introduction

Confronted with the name of Peadar O'Donnell, the man in the street in Ireland might be "stretched"—as the vernacular has it—to say if he was best known as a writer or as a political figure. "The greatest agitator of his generation" is how Bowyer Bell, the American author of what is virtually the authorized history of Ireland's IRA, describes him in *The Secret Army*. Any of those who witnessed Peadar in the 1930s haranguing a hostile crowd from the top of a lamppost in the center of Dublin might be inclined to agree. But there must be many young Irish readers, as well as non-Irish ones, who have enjoyed *Islanders* or *The Big Windows* without being conscious of any political overtones. Peadar himself might share the man in the street's dilemma. At an early stage of life he set himself deliberately to learn the craft of writing. Yet perhaps even then, as certainly later, he regarded his pen as a weapon to achieve political ends. We shall find the two activities closely interwoven at most periods of his life. Any attempt to assess Peadar O'Donnell's contribution to twentieth-century Irish culture must clearly take into account both elements.

A striking feature of the revolutionary periods in modern Ireland has been their impact on imaginative literature. Conversely, an outsider wishing to appreciate what it felt like to be an Irishman at such times (and remember it is how men feel, not what men think, that determines how men act) will reach this understanding most easily through certain poems of Yeats, the early plays of O'Casey, the short stories of the young Sean O'Faolain and Frank O'Connor, and some of the novels of Liam O'Flaherty and Peadar O'Donnell. Speaking personally, I can say that when I read *The Knife* as a young man, I had my first inkling of the reality behind the clash of intransigent Republicanism in Ireland and the early supporters of the Irish Free State.

But O'Donnell is also a regional novelist of unusual quality. He wrote six novels, every one of them set against the background of his native remote and rural Donegal. He describes in these a way of life which is— or rather, was, since the coming of the motorcar, television, and the tourist have now adulterated it for ever—unique in Europe. A handful of other Irish writers have handled this material. Peig Sayers and Tomas O Crohan wrote autobiographies in Irish, which have been translated, vividly describing the lives lived by themselves and those like them on the Greater Blasket island at the southwest tip of County Kerry. O Crohan states proudly that his purpose is to leave some record behind "for the like of us will never be again." O'Donnell is a more sophisticated writer than either of these, and he writes directly in English; but he has the same ear for the subtle or vivid phrase—often stemming from the Gaelic—the same firsthand knowledge of the unsentimental shrewdness of the peasant that lies behind, and when his fiction touches politics, which is history in the making, he knows the forces that drive men to action.

O'Donnell's nearest literary relative is Liam O'Flaherty. O'Flaherty was an Aran islander, like O'Donnell obsessed with a determination to write. He first wrote in Irish, soon changed to English, then returned to writing in Irish in later life. All his stories and many of his novels relate to the same small townland communities O'Donnell writes of, and sometimes a passage relating to them might have come from the pen of either writer. But O'Flaherty is a more impressionist, individualistic, romantic writer than O'Donnell. When he describes a man's actions, it is as if he drew with charcoal, and when he writes of animals in his stories, he feels his way inside the beasts, so that we experience the terror of the little seagull learning to fly, the playfulness, the lazy sensuousness, the make-believe ferocity of the kitten first being taught by its mother how to hunt. For O'Donnell the farmyard animals, though vividly described, are part of the village scene—perhaps he reflects Catholic teaching that they are created only for man's use. O'Flaherty is probably the greater literary artist; but his very gifts, his excitability, sometimes lead him astray, so that he will tire of a story, bundle it to an end and throw it aside when his characters get out of hand. O'Donnell's resolution is quite different.

He has the same respect for character expressing itself in forceful action—The Knife, Nuala, or Sam Rowan might be O'Flaherty personages—but he has a stronger sense of community. When he draws a story to a close, a social purpose has been realized—though this is far from suggesting didacticism.

Two of Peadar O'Donnell's autobiographical volumes concern phases of the Irish struggle, while the third concerns the Spanish civil war, though this too returns to an Irish setting. In the development of modern Ireland two political traditions combine and conflict: on the one hand the constitutionalism of British democracy, which enabled Irishmen like Burke, O'Connell, and Parnell to learn the parliamentary game, and paved the way for their successors to set up a closely similar system of government in Dublin; on the other, that of the oath-bound secret societies— the Macedonian revolutionaries, the *carbonari* of Italy, whose counterpart in Ireland is the Fenian tradition of the Irish Republican Brotherhood and the modern IRA. A third tradition has sometimes entered, but it has seldom dominated. The vision of human brotherhood is present in Wolfe Tone at the end of the eighteenth century and in Connolly's teaching prior to the Easter Rising of 1916; but it is only recessively represented in between, in the agitation of Lalor and Davitt, and it has been conspicuous by absence since. The kaleidoscopic intricacies of Irish politics may best be understood if it is recalled that the hard-core nationalist militancy of the Fenians was being constantly tempted and eroded by the respectability of the parliamentarians on the one side—hence the split over the Treaty in 1921 and de Valera's founding of a constitutional party in 1926, and the demand for a social policy on the other. Peadar O'Donnell was a militant in the IRA who was never tempted by constitutionalism. But he did believe the IRA should serve a socialist, as well as a nationalist end, and after abortive struggles within the leadership he and two comrades led a short-lived splinter group outside in the mid-1930s. Thereafter his role as a social publicist was confined to addressing a multiplicity of public meetings and the long series of articles and editorials in *The Bell*. His was a voice in the wilderness, because in these years Ireland was one of the most conservative states in Europe. Toward the end of the 1960s, however, there was a fresh interest in leftist thinking in Irish life. It is possible that when the record of recent times comes to be written, O'Donnell will appear a seminal figure, a forerunner.

However that may be, whatever he wrote in the political field has always literary value. *The Gates Flew Open* adds something to the select prison literature of all lands. *Salud!* catches an aspect of the Spanish war that only a novelist who had himself lived through revolutionary times in a peasant country could catch.

This small book could never have taken its actual form without the generous assistance and recollections of O'Donnell himself, and also that of several of his friends, some of whom are mentioned by name in the text. Obviously it is far from an authorized "Life"; perhaps that will come. I have tried to keep my own views of politics to a minimum; but where Irishmen are concerned, interpretations will out—and where they do, I must emphasize that they are mine, and not Peadar's own.

Peadar O'Donnell

1

The Formative Years

Peadar O'Donnell was born on February 22, 1893, at Meenmore near the village of Dungloe on the sea-coast of County Donegal, the most northwesterly county of Ireland. Historically, Donegal forms part of the province of Ulster, which is the part of Ireland having the shortest sea-passage to Britain. From the seventeenth century onwards this whole region was colonized extensively by English and Scotch settlers, who were stalwart upholders of the reformed religion. In 1922, six of the more easterly Ulster counties were detached to remain under Britain, when the rest of Ireland, including Donegal, became independent under the Dublin government. But even in Donegal there was a mixed population, most of the richer farms being in settlers' hands, while the native, usually Catholic, Irish held the outlying hill-farms.

The O'Donnells were among these. Peadar's father had a farm of five acres—and a range of rough mountain grazing with it. He was a migrant laborer. The pattern

of his life, as of many of his neighbors, was to take
agricultural work in Scotland during the summer, returning home in October. During the winter months
he managed the local corn-kiln, which was owned by
the village landlord. Though the sea was nearby and
he owned a boat, this was not a source of income. Often
he would take the family out rod- or line-fishing, but
only "for the pot." Daybreak or sunset were the best
times for this. The family lived a thrifty, active life.

There were nine children, of whom Peadar was the
fifth. Two brothers and two sisters are buried in
America. Another sister was living in Cleveland in the
1970s. It was the youngest son, Barney, who eventually
took over the farm. In contrast to sturdier farming communities, where the land would afford the father to
keep on the eldest son as co-worker and ultimate heir,
this has long been the tradition in the Irish west.

English was the language of the home by this date,
but Irish was not far back. The children picked it up
naturally from their grandparents and the older people
around. Under the British occupation, Irish was, of
course, frowned on, and Peadar remembers his father
telling him he had been beaten at school for speaking
Irish.

The land of the farm at Meenmore runs straight
down to the Atlantic, and there is still a miniature
rough-stone harbor. To the west one can see the islands
of Aranmore and Innisfree, where Peadar later taught.
A little inland to the east lies Deryhenny, where he
had his second school. The whole district is known as

The Rosses, and the father is still remembered as "the greatest musicianer of The Rosses." Clearly it was a lively house, because where there is a musicianer in the house, neighbors will visit, and a chance occasion will spark off a night's jollification.

One of Peadar's vivid early memories is of going out fishing with his father in the dark and impatiently waiting for the dawn. It always seemed maddeningly slow in coming. Later in jail, long hours of solitary confinement, waiting for either release or execution, were to provide a parallel experience and to throw his thoughts back to expressing in fiction the earlier impressions.

At the age of three, still in petticoats, Peadar went to the national school. The schoolhouse was next door, so no doubt it was an easy way to get the child out of the house. "You're a great man," said the teacher when the new scholar first made his appearance. "I am," came the prompt answer, with the cheeky, but disarming self-confidence that the future writer-revolutionary was to retain to the end of his days.

Other children left school at 14. Peadar must have been a promising student, because he was kept on as a monitor. Then, at the age of 18, he was sent to St. Patrick's, the teacher-training college in Drumcondra, Dublin. In 1913 he returned to his native Donegal as a teacher in his own right. He spent periods at Innisfree and at Deryhenny on the mainland, and was then transferred to the island school at Aranmore. This is one of the larger islands off the Irish coast and is still

quite thickly populated. In 1918 it held 300 families
and their progeny filled two schools and kept a total of
nine teachers busy.

Peadar's teaching methods were already revolutionary, far ahead of his time. They were remembered
vividly half a century later by one of his first pupils,
Hugh O'Hara of Chicago. He described how one of
the scholars was caught "hiding out" from school.
Peadar seldom beat a boy—a rare abstention in Ireland
even today. Instead, he set up a school court to try the
offender, and for two days prosecuting attorney and
defense attorney called witnesses and argued before an
elected judge. There was a policeman and even an
executioner on call, in case his services were required.
History does not recall the verdict.

It was on Aranmore that Peadar first began writing.
He set himself a regular stint of one hour. He had in
mind a possible career as journalist. But he was also,
he says, obsessed with a fetish: pure English. None of
this early work was ever submitted for publication. But
when his first books did appear, the style showed the
bareness and clarity of journalism, without the clichés.
It would be hard to discern literary "influences." The
beauty revealed derives directly from the subject matter,
not from literary artifice.

It was while teaching on Aranmore also that O'Donnell's second great interest manifested itself. A visit to
Scotland introduced him to socialist ideas. At that time
Donegal laborers migrating seasonally to Britain "lived
rough" on the Scottish farms. Initially they showed no
great enthusiasm for agitation to improve their con-

ditions, and Peadar realized why. He knew that these men were realists. They went with one object—to earn as much money as they could to bring home for the winter months. The spring sowing in, and the turf cut, they would be off again. They accepted conditions in the bothies as British soldiers accepted conditions in the trenches in what was then known as the Great War. Many even realized that a plentiful shake of clean straw on a barn floor was a healthier bed than a mattress that had been stored in a shed for the damp winter months. Later, Joe Duncan, as secretary of the Farm Workers' Union, was to campaign for, and secure social legislation to improve conditions. But what appealed to Peadar was the wider vision of power transferred to a government of the working class, a vision he learned from the talk in Glasgow of men like Willie Galagher, soon to become first communist Member in the British Parliament, Emanuel Shinwell, another radical M.P., and John MacLean. This radical demand for workers' power links Ireland with the anarcho-syndicalist tradition of Scotland, Italy, and Spain, and is in striking contrast to the campaign for day-to-day improvement that is the staple of the socialist movement in England and America. Bernadette Devlin in the Ulster of 1970 echoes the witness Peadar offered two generations earlier. As a trade-union organizer, O'Donnell had later to temporize, as did the communists, with the more materialistic socialist teaching, but the end-vision remained unchanged.

In 1917 or 1918 Peadar determined to leave schoolteaching and take up the career of political agitator.

He obtained a full-time post organizing for the Irish Transport and General Workers' Union. This was paid work, four pounds ten shillings a week, which was actually better than his teacher's salary. The job took him all through the northeastern counties—Tyrone, Derry, Armagh, Monaghan—and also into Belfast. One of his first campaigns involved industrial action among the workers at the Monaghan county mental hospital. This was a stay-in strike, a new revolutionary principle. Peadar had noted that the attendants of a nearby hospital had forfeited public sympathy when they simply walked out on strike. He himself acted as Governor of the hospital while the strike lasted and saw that the patients were well cared for. After twelve days the strikers' demands were met.

At this time O'Donnell knew none of the political leaders in other parts of the country. Just as today many west-of-Ireland parishes have closer ties with London, Manchester, Cleveland, or the Bronx, Donegal had closer ties with Scotland than with Dublin. Peadar saw James Connolly, the socialist leader who was executed in 1916, twice, but never spoke with him. On both occasions Connolly faced a hostile crowd. The first time, he was speaking from a suffragette platform, jeered at by his audience, many of them working men like himself. The second occasion he was encountering catcalls as a "bandy-legged militiaman" from a crowd of women as he led his small Irish Citizen Army through Dublin streets. Jim Larkin, the fiery workers' leader during the great lockout of 1913, O'Donnell did not meet until 1925. It was at the house of Delia Larkin, Jim's sister, that Peadar met Sean O'Casey during the truce period in 1922.

O'Casey had been a member of the Irish Citizen Army, but his subsequent sneering attitude toward Connolly for his involvement with the national movement did not appeal to O'Donnell. Peadar also frankly admits that he failed to recognize O'Casey's genius. He attributed this failure to O'Casey's weak eyesight; normally, Peadar would claim, genius shines to the world through dynamic eyes.

Peadar was soon to endorse the identification Connolly had made: British imperialism and property capitalism were the twin oppressors of the Irish working class. The struggle for freedom must be waged against both simultaneously. This was the struggle Wolfe Tone had urged just over a century earlier—the men of no property as the backbone for insurgent republicanism. By 1919 Peadar was fully committed to the Volunteers and the physical-force movement in the fighting that was spreading all over the country and was to lead on to the emergence, after centuries of eclipse, of an independent Irish state. The following year he resigned from the Irish Transport and General Workers' Union, which he felt was repudiating the tactics of Connolly's Citizen Army, and joined the Irish Republican Army.

2

Revolutionary Nationalist

When Patrick Pearse's little band of 500 men marched out in 1916 to seize the principal buildings of Dublin, they appeared isolated and unknown. They were quickly defeated and their leaders executed. But even before the grisly episode of Connolly's end, a movement was afoot to raise sympathy with their stand. This joined forces with, and revitalized, Arthur Griffith's movement known as Sinn Fein, and in 1918 fought the general election on explicit rejection of all British claims to rule Ireland and a pledge to use force to eliminate this. In all counties except the six northeastern ones, Sinn Fein won a substantial victory.

Before long, fresh fighting developed. This time the revolutionaries did not repeat the mistake of trying to hold public buildings where they could be surrounded and smashed by superior, well-organized forces. Guerilla warfare was the pattern. (It is worth remembering that there were no recent precedents for this in 1918. The Irish had to innovate and improvise.) The general policy was to have as few full-time fighters as possible. It was more effective if men went about their ordinary, bread-earning operations by day, then organized to strike silently under cover of darkness.

Once a revolutionary was identified and known to police or military, however, he had to leave home and go "on the run." This often meant sleeping out on the hills, though there were also many houses in the country villages where patriots could count on shelter, food, and sometimes a reliable watch for British raiding parties while they snatched needed sleep. Strangely, in the light of later history, many of these houses were Protestant. The local "Orangemen," as Ulster Protestants are generally called, might not sympathize with the rebels, but they would not inform on neighbors to the British. There were, of course, also many Orangemen who did take a more partisan line and later joined the "B" Specials organized by the Northern Unionists to oppose Home Rule. But these houses were known. It is this curious cross-current of loyalties that is embodied in the character of Sam Rowan in *The Knife*. Sam Rowan had frequent prototypes in real life.

Peadar O'Donnell's first military action was when, still an organizer of the local I.T.G.W.U., he took part in the capture of the police barracks in the small village of Ballytreane. Around this time, by the roadside in County Monaghan, the republican oath was administered to him. By this, he pledged himself to "support and defend the Irish Republic and the Government of the Irish Republic, which is Dail Eireann, against all enemies, foreign and domestic. . . ." Dail Eireann was the revolutionary parliament set up in Dublin after the 1918 election. Later, after the Treaty split, those who opposed the majority vote in Dail Eireann supporting it pledged themselves to the Republic and to the Army Executive Council.

In 1920 Peadar had resigned his trade-union post to serve full time in the IRA without salary. He had to live off the country—"on the run" and in constant danger of arrest.

Military rank was not very precisely defined at this period of the fighting, but operational territory was. If a unit in one area required help for a particular "job," this had to be requested through the command hierarchy, to prevent confusion on the ground and the chance of being caught prematurely in a round-up provoked by another unit's activity. The Northern Division of the Volunteers had four brigades. Peadar was in command of the 2nd. A younger brother, Frank, was vice-brigadier of the 1st, and during the civil war became brigadier. A third brother, Joe ("the toughest of the three of us," according to Peadar), was engaged in making bombs and explosive devices.

Peadar's charge consisted of five Battalions, drawn from men who held regular jobs by day, and a Flying Column—full-time men operating "on the run." Their territory stretched from Malin Head, the most northerly point in Ireland, across to Fanad Head and down to Lifford and Glendowan. For a short time Derry city was included. Brigade activity included demolition of bridges and general sabotage, ambushing police patrols, shooting up trains bringing reinforcements, and rescue of captured comrades.

In May 1921 a British destroyer put in unexpectedly at Burtonport, near the O'Donnell home farm, and managed to arrest the whole Divisional Staff in a major round-up. Peadar narrowly escaped on this occasion, but shortly afterwards he was wounded in the shoulder in another action. He managed to keep running and subsequently to convalesce in a friendly house in the Brockagh mountains, another experience that helped inspire a novel—*The Big Windows*. Peadar was never captured by the British, though a comrade who received a leg wound in the same action was. In a different encounter O'Donnell received a light flesh wound in the leg.

In July 1921, news of the cease-fire reached Donegal, causing local bewilderment. Few believed it meant peace. Peadar preferred to regard it as a breathing-space that would give opportunity for intensive training. The Flying Column was broken up. These were the men who had had the most fighting experience, and they were distributed to help organize others. Instructors in new arms and techniques arrived from Dublin, including Tod Andrews, then a commerce student, later to become one of the most dynamic leaders of the new Irish economy. The main training camp was established at a wealthy Englishman's shooting-lodge near Letterkenny.

Many of the Donegal Volunteers were eager to carry on fighting. When rumors came that the London peace talks were going badly, they were almost welcome. "We didn't get much of a chance last time. Maybe we'll get a chance now," was a typical comment from one young recruit. News that the Treaty with the British, conceding only part of the insurrectionaries' demands, had actually been signed caused real dismay.

The period following the signing of the Treaty is a tragic one in Irish history. In Donegal, as in other parts of the country, it was also a confused one. Comrades-in-arms who had fought together against the British now had to decide whether they would follow Griffith and Collins in accepting a compromise or de Valera's somewhat ambiguous lead in rejecting the Treaty, with its virtually inevitable corollary of renewed fighting not only against the British, but against those who had accepted it. The voting in the southern Irish parliament, now meeting for the first time in open session, was close: 64 for, 57 against. Give or take ten percent, the division among the Donegal volunteers was the same.

It is tempting in retrospect to look on the post-Treaty split as a left-wing, right-wing alignment. But this is hardly accurate. Certainly the outcome of the civil war was to consolidate a conservative, property-respecting, if not always property-owning, Irish Free State. Some believed sincerely this was best for the country, some believed it was the best they could get, some probably had an eye to the main chance. The shopkeepers in the main went Treatyite. The Church too was for it, with few exceptions. But the outlook of the men who opposed varied just as widely. Many were radicals. But

Erskine Childers, one of the most intransigent, was a man of wealth and English lineage. De Valera was far from being a radical. Austin Stack, a solicitor, held strong right-wing views, yet opposed the Treaty. Many of the men on the ground were loath to concern themselves with "politics." They had taken an oath of loyalty to the Republic, they had killed in its defense. As Peadar often liked to put it subsequently: "They just were not able to come down off the high ground of the Republic to the low level of the Treaty: the sort that martyrs are made of, not revolutionaries."

Peadar himself, of course, was a convinced socialist whose attitude inside the national movement had been one of impatience to get rid of the British in order to have a free hand to improve the country. Popular radicalism in Donegal was strong enough to ensure that even local dances ended with singing Connolly's socialist *Watchword of Labour,* rather than the classless nationalism of *The Soldier's Song.* But the clearest mind of all, according to Peadar, among those who opposed the Treaty was that of the Galway man Liam Mellows. Though Mellows himself was not a socialist, but merely, again in Peadar's words "a good Fenian radical," it was his intuitive, near-Marxist analysis of the social forces that underlay the seeming random alignment of individuals on the Treaty issue that clarified Peadar's own views. When he got to know Mellows well in Mountjoy jail, he regretted that these arguments had not been fully developed in debates before the Army Convention, where they might have induced greater realism. He persuaded Mellows to set them down in *Notes from Mountjoy Jail*. Mellows, aged 30, was one of the four Republican leaders executed in Machiavellian ruthlessness by the Free State government on December 8, 1922.

While the great debate over ratification of the Treaty continued throughout the country, a jockeying for position was taking place among the army units. Many republicans felt the best hope of healing the split lay in forcing a renewal of fighting with the British forces, which were now withdrawing from the twenty-six southern counties but consolidating themselves in the northeastern six. If this happened, it was felt the Free State forces would hardly dare side openly with the British against their own former comrades. Skirmishing took place at Pettigo and Belleek, where the Donegal border marches with that of Derry and Fermanagh counties.

Peadar was in close touch with the situation in Donegal, but most of his time was now spent in Dublin, where he was serving with Commandant-General's rank on the Republican Army Executive. Headquarters were in the Four Courts of Justice, and Peadar was there on June 28, 1922, when the Free State forces bombarded it and thus launched the first full operation of the civil war. When the building exploded in flames two days later, Peadar was among the prisoners taken. Republicans so captured were not formally tried and sentenced, but were interned while the fighting lasted. Before long, some were to be taken out and shot by way of reprisal. Peadar knew this might be his fate at any moment, particularly since he had a brother known to be commanding a unit of the anti-Treatyites.

The Free State authorities in fact kept Peadar constantly on the move: first Mountjoy jail, then Tintown, the Curragh camp, the Curragh "glasshouse" (military prison), Mountjoy again, Finner, Mountjoy, Arbour Hill, Mountjoy, Kilmainham, Mountjoy, the Curragh.

But on March 16, 1924, he escaped from the Curragh. *The Gates Flew Open,* which is Peadar's account of his jail experiences, gives a cryptic account of this event that ended them, which might lead the reader to suspect that a lady was involved, particularly since he refers earlier to corresponding with sympathizers outside through the intermediary of a Miss Lile O'Donel. In truth, however, the reference is to a friendly Free State soldier, whose name could not be revealed at the time.

Be that as it may, romance was not far off. On June 25, 1924, Peadar O'Donnell married Lile O'Donel in the Eccles Street parish church in Dublin. It was a modest, intimate ceremony attended by about twenty guests, among them Mrs. de Valera, who was a friend of Lile, and Dr. Paddy Browne, a fine Gaelic scholar, later President of University College, Galway.

Miss O'Donel's father had owned a landlord's estate near Foxford in County Mayo, but sided with Parnell and supported the "no rent" campaign against his own material interest in the 1880s. Later, after the British parliament passed the Land Acts to allow tenants to purchase their farms through the Irish Land Commis-

sion by means of small annual payments spread over
the years, he sold his estate to the Land Commission.
He was also a member of the Irish Republican Brotherhood that planned the Rising of 1916. Lile by all
accounts combined a childish gaiety with utter fear-
lessness. While her future husband was in jail, she once
thrust her way into the office of a prominent supporter
of the Free State, Tom Johnson, the Labour leader,
warned him to his face that if anything happened to
Peadar, he himself would not be alive that night, and
stalked out. She and her two sisters had all been left
wealthy in their own right and henceforward Peadar
had no material wants. But he was never made pom-
pous or corrupted by wealth.*

It was a lastingly happy marriage, until Lile's death
in 1969. They had no children, but adopted one son,
also Peadar.

O'Donnell himself was elected to the Dail while he
was still in jail. But it was an empty formula, since
Republican policy was not to claim their seats in what
they regarded as a puppet parliament upheld only by
traitors and British might.

---

*On one occasion, around 1939, R. B. McDowell, a fine scholar and
later a Fellow of Dublin University, then an undergraduate student,
called with a delegation on the revolutionary writer to ask him to be
one of the speakers at the Historical Society's inaugural. "Of course,
Mr. O'Donnell," piped McDowell nervously, when the preliminaries
were settled, "everybody on the platform will be in evening dress." "Oh
no, they won't," answered Peadar promptly, "because I won't."

3

The Early Novels

Peadar O'Donnell had spent twenty-one months in jail. The days were lively enough, as we shall see in the discussion below of the autobiographical volume, *The Gates Flew Open,* which he devoted to this experience. There were classes to be organized to uphold the morale of young prisoners, constant planning for an escape, and endless discussions with fellow-revolutionaries on the political and economic aspects of the struggle outside. But this was also the period when O'Donnell settled down seriously to his other vocation, that of an imaginative writer. As soon as it was possible to resume a more settled life outside, his first novels appeared.

Storm is his first book. It carries the subtitle "A Story of the Irish War." Part of it was written in jail. Another section was written in the station waiting-room at Portadown, waiting for the Dublin connection just after his escape from jail. It was published in Dublin by the Talbot Press. No date appears on this volume, but it seems to have been issued in 1925 or '26.

The storm of the title is the great Atlantic gale that struck the west coast of Ireland on November 12, 1919, and also the revolutionary struggle ripening in Ireland at the same period. The book has the unadorned simplicity of a young man's work. It would be absurd to praise it highly and it is equally unnecessary to dismiss it patronizingly. It is a plain, robust story, and we may suspect that the exercises Peadar wrote when pursuing his "fetish for pure English" while schoolmastering on Aranmore, and subsequently destroyed, were something like this. Nevertheless, it foreshadows in two respects the characteristics that were to distinguish O'Donnell's work both as writer and social reformer. The first is his unerring observation of countrymen and the country scene. Here is a father's farewell to his son who has joined the rebels and has to go "on his keeping" in the hills:

> And now a silent, solemn parting, whispered prayers and words of farewell. Sean Mor, big, strong man that he was, had no word to say to his hunted son—just a handshake, and he stooped abruptly on his oar, the others getting quickly to their places. Like a ghost the boat drew away from the shore and merged in the gloom. Eamonn and Charlie Beag stole up the fields, making for the mountains, that were piled like clouds along the edge of the sky.

The second is his knowledge of the details of poverty, which naturally arouse pity. Yet simultaneously comes the realization that this poverty strengthens sympathy among neighbors, whom affluence would divide. The central character in the book is an island schoolmaster, almost certainly part-autobiographical, who is also one of Ireland's first freedom fighters. Here is how Eamonn explains to the young woman teacher who has come in from the mainland the facts of rural life and the implications of poverty:

> They talked of the hardships of poor children in mountain districts. Eamonn explained that, in his opinion, the incident that had the greatest effect on his life took place when a young companion, who hadn't fivepence for a fourth book, lay out on the mountain for days—it was March and there were showers of hail, and he had no boots—until his mother who was gathering a churning in cupfuls, had enough cream collected to make a pound or two of butter. She took the butter to a shop, bought a few eatables, adjusting her bill so that there would be a few pence change coming, and then the boy got his new book. That memory stuck. He was always afraid some of the children in the school might be lying about the hills, because they hadn't the money for a new book.
> "Life is very drab, surely, for the people here," Maire said thoughtfully. "It must be almost unbearable."
> "No, you are not right in that, I think," Eamonn suggested. "There is the strongest sympathy knitting them all together. It is difficult for a stranger to see. Have you ever noticed how the hardest pressed of them would somehow manage to spare a naggin of milk when a neighbour's cow was dry, or there was a sick child in the house?"

Peadar was to spend much of his lifetime propagating schemes to alleviate the poverty of the western districts. Did he accept that affluence must make its inroads on the human qualities he admired so highly? The dilemma is one that faces every social reformer.

The incidents that make up *Islanders* (1927), Pea-

dar's second published book, were also written in jail
and smuggled out by a friendly Free State officer. Later
incidents were written out while "on the run" after
the escape from the Curragh. There was no cobbling.
Liam O'Flaherty, whom O'Donnell first met at a socialist meeting in Liberty Hall during these days, sent
the manuscript to his own publisher, Jonathan Cape,
where Cape's reader, Edward Garnett, accepted it immediately. Perhaps O'Donnell is unique as a writer in
never having collected a rejection slip. Reviews too
were ecstatic, when it appeared, both from the "quality" Sunday papers and from the popular press. Robert
Lynd contributed an introduction in which he praised
O'Donnell's power to create a whole family of characters, as distinct from merely inventing them.

Reading the book today, we are aware of a slight
scrappiness and an occasional non sequitur amid the
short chapters, perhaps arising from the manner in
which it was composed. The sense of nostalgia for the
open-air life also stems undoubtedly from the writer's
finding himself jailed in solitary confinement. But there
is no longer anything amateur in the writing.

The opening of *Islanders* vividly evokes dawn on the
western seaboard, echoing, as already suggested, an
experience the author knew well as a small boy:

> Daybreak spread wearily over the mountains to the east,
> and crept down into the misty waste. A thin breeze chilled
> the ebb-tide. Loose bodyless clouds released a drizzle of
> rain. Inniscara Island shivered in the cold-lipped Atlantic,
> indifferent to a dawn that was lifeless.

We meet the Doogan family and witness their hard struggle to wrest a living—their few hens, whose eggs are painstakingly assembled on the dresser until they form the dozen that can be taken to the shop to be exchanged for the grain of tea or tobacco; the carefully watched cow; the fishing when the herring is in; the occasional poaching; in one instance the theft of a bag of flour when the family faces utter starvation. It is interesting to note that the latter is in no sense here a revolutionary act. It is in strict conformity with Catholic social teaching that theft by a starving man is no theft, and it is defended tersely by Charlie Doogan: "it was rightly come by." But as soon as the family can afford it, it is carefully paid for, and even on her deathbed the mother seeks reassurance that this has been done.

The whole framework of the book, in fact, reflects the simple, unquestioning religious faith of the Irish countryside, a faith that still survives today in many places, though seldom with the same strength and resignation. The family is the unit. The mother slaves and stints to rear her children. When her time comes to die, she is still concerned for the household animals, for life's sustenance depends on them, then for her children to be gathered about her. The boat has been sent for the priest; meanwhile she rambles:

> "What was I sayin'?" she said, struggling to concentrate. "Sure I saw the hens finish their feed meself. Don't let the black cow get a shower of rain," she continued after a pause, "an' it her first day out. An' it must be time to give the calf his drink." . . .

When the boat was seen returning Mary Manus spoke
to her.

"How d'ye think ye are now, Mary?"

"I'm very weak."

"Maybe ye might as well have the priest," she said.

"He'll be welcome," Mary said. "It's only good he can
do. Maybe me work is o'er, Mary. Well, welcome be the
will of God. I can leave them now easier. Gather them
all round me, Mary, a chailleach." Then she seemed to
pass into a slumber.

The priest arrives and anoints her for death. And then:

"Yon flour, Charlie?"

"I paid for it, first week of the herrin'."

"That's good, Charlie, that's good. . . . God bless Charlie,
poor mother never reared a better son."

It is tempting to believe that Rousseau's dream of
the noble savage has some reality in the lives of these
folk. Life has its frustrations, particularly for Charlie,
who frets that his hard work and great strength frequently bring home nothing at all. Yet his horizon is
limited and in the end he too has the faith to accept.
The free-for-all of the rat-race of modern civilization
belongs to another world.

By the time he came to write *Adrigoole,* which was
published in 1929, Peadar was operating in more com-
fortable circumstances. Married to Lile, he was living
at his first Dublin home in Marlborough Road, south
of the Liffey. Later on they moved north to 176 Upper
Drumcondra Road, a smallish semi-detached house,
simply but comfortably furnished, the walls chock-a-

block with modern Irish paintings, which was to be his home for the remainder of his life.

The origins of this book were twofold. A story appeared in a Dublin newspaper, the *Irish Independent,* of a mother and child who had been found dead from starvation, surrounded by other famished children, in a small farmhouse in a remote part of the Cork-Kerry border. They had been ostracized by their neighbors on account of their republican sympathies in the late civil war. The husband, desperate from poverty, had been caught on his first brewing of *poteen,* the illicit alcohol, and, unable to pay the fine, which the seasoned operator merely regards as part of the business expenses, had been jailed for twelve months. Meanwhile the family starved to their death.

The second aspect of the book's origin was a reflective realization of what the light-hearted billeting of rebel troops during the revolutionary war had meant to farms close to the poverty line. Their feeding, cheerfully and willingly given, had mortgaged many a small farm's future. In *There Will be Another Day,* O'Donnell tells us:

> I escaped from prison in March 1924. I made my way to Donegal and took shelter for a few weeks in mountain townlands. I often walked alone in the shadow of the hills. It was then that the sense of gloom and doom in my novel, *Adrigoole,* entered my mind. It disturbed me to recall how often I had billeted a considerable number of men on these homes in the Tan days. I was more aware now of the weakness of this economy. My eyes were sharper. I noticed how the heather ate its way into land

that had fallen into feeble hands. It saddened me that
mountains should renew their grip on fields that had
been won from them by desperate, hopeful men.

Anyone who has witnessed the subsistence economy of
western Ireland will know what this means. In the rich
midlands, the saying has it, the land keeps the farmer;
in the congested west, the farmer keeps the land.

As in *Islanders,* poverty, and its accompanying neighborliness, pride, and struggle, provide the central
themes of *Adrigoole.* The Cork-Kerry tragedy has been
transposed to a Donegal setting where the author is at
home with the landscape and its people. Here is the
landscape:

> rocks were sharp-edged, deep-rooted, broad-faced; the
> patches of soil were twisted around granite boulders;
> there were no ploughs, only spades; no horses, only
> donkeys. . . . And the farms were tasselled at the moun-
> tain boundary with roots of heather that pushed down-
> ward; eating downward, waiting for the men below to
> weaken; waiting; to go back without feeling from a push
> upward, and then again to wait. . . .

The sense of the bog as a brooding, malevolent being
permeates the book:

> "It's the bog underneath," Hughie said; "it's hard to
> drive bog deep, an' it sucks an' sucks at any strong life
> above it. I'm gettin' I could spit on bog anywhere I see
> it, even at the bottom of a drain.". . .
> "D'ye mind the first summers, an' the blaze an' the life
> that was in everythin'? I'd be frightened if I thought
> Adrigoole was goin' agin' us."
> "With all the rain, the bog is movin' up," Hughie said.

"If ye make a bog a thing that moves an' deadens an' has meanin' ye'll frighten me, Hughie."

We meet the people of this landscape at the "hiring fair" at Strabane, where the children of the small farms are sent when grown. The wealthy farmers of the nearby Lagan eye them like cattle before buying their labor, as negro slaves were once bought in the Deep South:

"Tommy, mon, are ye back?" a farmer greeted Tommy. Tommy looked up and was silent. "Well, mon, I hae a laddie already. But, hi, Sam." Sam, a youngish, tall farmer, dandered over. "There's yer laddie," he said, indicating Tommy.

"He's no vera likely lookin'," Sam demurred. "I took twa terms out o' him," the other urged. "A good riser?" Sam inquired. "He's no by hissel', but whistle an' he's up smart as a dog."

Boys go the the Lagan, and return as men, filled with memories of the prosperous rolling fields, the heavy-footed horses, the well-filled granaries. Yet the homeland draws. "Oh the grip, oh the grip of irregular fields," the poet Patrick Kavanagh wrote of the neighboring county of Monaghan. Many earn money in the Lagan to go to Scotland, in Scotland save money for a passage to America, and in America earn cash to buy a small homestead in Adrigoole. Hughie Dalach's odyssey is shortened by good fortune. His Brigid has a bachelor uncle, Neddie Brian, who owns a farm. All three meet unexpectedly at a wake, just as the two younger ones are planning their way to America. "I have a place for Brigid and for her man, an' she made good choosing in you," Neddie Brian tells Hughie. Sometimes O'Donnell's telling of an incident borders on pathos, but the shrewd knowledge of country ways and the unerring ear for dialogue saves it from sentimentalization.

So Hughie and Brigid settle in Adrigoole. They labor and slave as they never did in the Lagan, Neddie Brian is happy, they are blessed with children. But relentlessly the bog waits. The "troubled times" come. Soldiers from the republican army tap on the window at night, are fed, housed, and there are cheerful stories and songs round the fire. But the food stocks dwindle. The truce intervenes, bringing hopes of a respite. But these hopes too dwindle. The new, bitter fighting of the civil war, dreaded by all, wished by none, comes. The Dalachs are on the side of the out-and-outers, the losing side. And so the book moves to its harrowing conclusion, the incident culled from a newspaper clipping.

The harshest irony is that it is Ireland's heroic fight for freedom that lays Adrigoole low. O'Donnell is not usually a gloomy author, but this is a very gloomy book. In speaking of it later, Peadar indicated that he felt he should have given it a different ending. Hughie Delach is too vigorous a character to have gone down in defeat in real life; he would have emigrated.

4
The Knife

More than any other of his books, Peadar was accustomed to say, the novel he published next, *The Knife* (1930), was "brewed from experience." The experience he had in mind was evidently twofold. Throughout his life O'Donnell was a lively observer of human nature, especially of the way in which a man's character is revealed under the test of a sudden crisis. A small incident, a brief sharp flare-up of violence, in the days when he was organizing a strike among the mental hospital workers of County Monaghan had made him aware of the solid strength behind the Northern Protestant temper. Ever afterwards he referred to them as "the only real fighters in Ireland"—as different from the volatile Southerners as Frenchmen are from Englishmen. During the war for independence, when his brigade covered east Donegal, he learned too of the deep cross-currents of neighborliness and loyalties, which often found the unwanted guest a safer billet in a politically opposed Protestant house than in a fear-crazed Catholic's.

The Knife is the most carefully constructed and dramatic of O'Donnell's novels. The surface narrative flows
with the ease of a well-plotted adventure story. But be-
neath the surface the book conveys with unusual veri-
similitude the political experience of the Irish war. We
witness the various characters choosing their stand in
response to the challenge of the times. Then, as history
moves on, we see these same characters molded by the
march of events, the Treaty, and the "Split" that followed it. On a smaller, simpler canvas, it is O'Donnell's
War and Peace. Just occasionally the construction may
seem over-neat: a character who correctly personifies a
trend in history may teeter on the edge of becoming a
marionette. But the drawing is never downright crude.
It is a broad truth that when men are blown off balance
by a revolutionary upheaval, the ideological stands they
take are influenced by both their private passions and
their material interests. To what extent they are candid
in admitting this to their colleagues, or even to themselves, is a debatable point. It is fair to say that the small
farmers, traders, and priests whom O'Donnell puts in
his book are far truer to life than the automatons who
sometimes appear in political fiction or drama. If challenged, he could probably cite a prototype from experience for each of the novel's characters.

The book opens with a colorful evocation of the
troubled past of Ireland's northern province which, as
has already been observed, was colonized early in the
seventeenth century by imported Protestant stock, the
native Irish of the older faith being driven to the bar-
ren hinterland. These Protestant settlers rallied to the

standard of William of Orange in 1690 to defend their grip on the land against James II and his Catholic allies in the siege of Derry and the battle of the Boyne. The Catholic Irish were defeated and forced back to the hills. The victors claimed King William as their hero and Orange as the symbol of their victory. For three subsequent centuries it was an annual event to see the Orangemen carry the banner of "King Billy of the Boyne" riding his white horse to victory, together with other anti-Papal emblems, in the parades of July 12. The Prologue to *The Knife* sums up this pageant of history thus:

> Three hundred years have piled up since that night and the crusted centuries entomb the misery of that flight which, even more than the centuries, dims the race memory of days of early greatness. The treeless hills now swarm with men and women and barelegged children on whose tongues still lives the language of the broken nation. A necklace of native farmers rings the hungry fringes of the plain, halting where the heather halts; the vibrant fields below are the booty of the planter. Back in the deepest reaches of the mountain tame natives serve the foreign landlord, and along the thickening veins of commerce native villages assemble around garrison posts.

The action of the book takes place in the Lagan valley on the eastern fringe of Donegal, where even today the two Irelands mingle, the rich lands still in Protestant hands, while those of the older faith strive to make a living from the mountainy farms:

The Lagan holds its lapful of strange children, planter

and native mixed, not fused, sweating together, thinking
apart, uneasy in silence, sudden in sidelong glances.

This, then, is the setting, a tightknit, but internally
tense, community, providing the background to the
more intimate drama that now unfolds.

A Catholic family, the Godfrey Dhus—father, two
sons, and redhead daughter ("a stubborn stiff-necked
breed the men, and a skinful of dynamite the woman"
is how a neighbour describes them) —have purchased
Montgomerys farm in what hitherto has been a solid
Protestant district. One by one we meet the local people
and witness their reaction to this event. The poorer
natives are triumphant to see one of their number bait-
ing the Orange lion. The local Catholic shopkeeper, Dan
Sweeney, is more wary. He smells a rival to the power
he has so carefully nurtured. "Dan's power had grown,"
the narrator observes, "because he had never pushed a
relative for anything; family-pushers narrow in their
base and topple sideways." The local priest is likewise
dubious. There are wild men on the Protestant side
who would burn the newcomers out; but they are held
in check by the toughest of the Orangemen, Sam Rowan
and his family. Rowan knows his ground and brings a
henchman, Billy White, to heel with the unprece-
dented threat of calling in the police to guard a Catholic home:

> "If ye burn Montgomerys where'll it end? The whole
> Lagan'll roast; them that has least can burn most."
> "An' is it leave them here to root and breed? Roast
> them now before they spread over the place like whins."

"I'll just tell the police and let them guard it." Billy
White stood aghast. "You'd never do that, Sammy, give
them a guard like a judge."
    "I'll just do that, Billy."

The most subtle character in the book, Doctor
Henry, is torn between both sides. A spell away from
home has given him a diffident, ironic detachment from
local loyalties. "I'm only a poor sort of Orangeman," he
says, "—my while in England kind of made an Irishman
of me. It's only at home an Orangeman is not Irish; in
England he'd beat the face off anybody who insisted he
was English." There is a moving, pleasant passage where
Doctor Henry calls at the Godfrey Dhus, both to warn
them of the trouble ahead from his own community
and, for his part, wryly to bid them welcome. He finds
Nuala Godfrey Dhu alone and the dialogue that ensues
is a good example of the light, bantering humor in
which O'Donnell excels:

> When he arrived at Montgomerys, Nuala chanced to
> be alone in the kitchen. She was flattening out a scone of
> oaten bread on the kitchen table. The Doctor rested a
> hand on the top of the door and leaned cross-legged
> against the edge.
>   "I'll bet you a shilling you break it," he said.
>   Nuala ran her hand under the wide, thin, circular,
> highly brittle cake, and raised it, and then revolving it
> round and round between her palms she brought it un-
> broken to the fire and stood it against the bread iron. Her
> face was flushed with the excitement of it, for she had been
> wondering whether she was capable of such a feat with
> so large sized a cake when the Doctor arrived. She turned
> with outstretched hand towards him, and he laid his
> shilling in her palm.

"I'll keep it for luck," she said, blowing on it.

"You're recruited to the Orangemen now," the Doctor said.

"Then you have your work before you to make them accept the recruit," she challenged.

"Ye have the truth there," the Doctor said gravely, "and I may as well say straight out I think it was looking for trouble to come here: not but you have a right to come in," he added.

"That's a big admission," Nuala said. "Won't you sit up and we will argue about it. Now tell me what the Orangemen are saying?" She was in dead earnest behind her banter, for she felt that only excited talk could have driven any Orangeman to such a step as this.

He delivers his warning in his diffident way, and perhaps he sees more clearly than Nuala with her passionate talk of freedom that basically the clash is a struggle for land and jobs, between the haves and the have nots, and that it would be better for all to sit down and share than to fight. She comments: "A body sees your mind; it's a damp, boggy kind of mind." In the end, he bids her welcome—"I'm likely to be the only Orangeman will do it"—and leaves her thoughtful.

Politics intervene. We move into the time of the war against the British. Not unnaturally, we find the family of Godfrey Dhu in the forefront on the national side. His two sons, The Knife and Hugh, are drilling and gun-running; Nuala is active as a courier. The Knife is a resolute and resourceful fighter. The local commandant of the Volunteers, James Burns, is more cautious. It is his brother who is the local priest and he himself is canvassing for local office as rate-collector. The whole family, in fact, is on the up—the women even wearing shoes or boots about the house in summer, as a neighbor caustically observes. Even more cautious and crafty is local-politician-shopkeeper-and-postmaster Dan Sweeney. He has an artful habit of calling on the old people to promise them their pension, as soon as he knows it's due anyway. He too supports the Volunteers, but only because he knows a change is coming. The Orangemen, of course, are opposed to the Volunteers, but at a certain point they too realize a change is coming. In a revealing debate among themselves they decide on a compact: if they are allowed to keep their property, they will concede the political power. This is, in fact, effectively the tactic adopted by the Southern Protestants after the Treaty settlement, though how many would have put it thus in words is impossible to tell.

This brings us to the second phase of the national struggle. The Treaty has been signed in London and the country divides. The stake-in-the-country men, the shopkeepers and place-hunters, are for the Treaty, and they have the support of the priests. In a fine, bitter scene Father Burns uses the pulpit to anathematize the out-and-outers who wish to fight on for the Republic. These include, of course, the Godfrey Dhus. The Knife invades the altar to protest at its being made a political platform, and Nuala shouts to the priest. "Shut your mouth, and go on with the prayers." This scene in the novel scandalized many when it was published, and it was virulently attacked by the clergy. Yet it reflected accurately a situation that arose in many parts of Ireland in 1922–23 and even later, when priests openly

talked politics from the altar and Republicans rose in
protest.

In the last chapters of the novel, the Knife has been
captured by the Free Staters. There are grim, but
boisterous days in jail. Then he is informed that he is
to be shot on what everyone knows is a trumped-up
charge. With him in arrest is Doctor Henry, in whose
house he had been found when on the run, and he too
is to be shot. There is only once chance of rescue. The
Republicans are defeated and powerless. The Orangemen of the Lagan could save the pair of them if they
would. Nuala goes to Sam Rowan, who has already
shown his sympathy and sense of fair play. The dialogue that ensues illustrates the dramatic skill O'Donnell often showed in his novels, yet, curiously, seemed
unable to muster when writing for the stage:

> Nuala walked up until only a pace separated them.
> "You could lead the Orangemen of the Lagan into a
> rescue," she said.
> "They think a lot of Doctor Henry," he agreed.
> "You could lead them into a rescue," she repeated.
> "There's some of them would put heed in what I'd say."
> "You could lead them into a rescue."
> "They would be willing to free the Doctor."
> "And does The Knife being with him, stop them?"
> "They would be a lot quicker if he was by himself."
> "Will it stop them?"
> "Are you asking me to rescue The Knife and Doctor
> Henry?"
> "As I never wanted to ask a thing in my life, Sam. But
> only if you can see that it can be done."
> "Orangemen could do a lot if they had their minds strong
> on it."
> "Then, Sam, you'll set their minds strong on it?"

"It won't be my fault if The Knife and Doctor Henry is shot," he said simply.

The rescue is carried out.

Nuala has no love but the Republic, but three men in the book are in love with her—James Burns, who turns against the Republic when she rejects him, and allows his personal spleen, bolstered by his place-seeking, to lead him to a venomous determination to exterminate The Knife; Doctor Henry, who accepts his failure with gentle melancholy; and Sam Rowan. Some readers may be reminded of the suitors of Isabel Archer in *The Portrait of a Lady*. The bold Sam Rowan carries the day; one would like to believe it a symbolic hope for the Ireland of the future.

Much of this book, in fact, for the thoughtful reader carries lessons for the understanding not only of the history of fifty years ago, but of later days—the romantic, passionate, dangerous idealism of the fighters for Irish nationhood, the incipient venality of those who first find themselves grasping at wealth or power, the hard struggle of level-headed men to prevent a divided community from tearing itself apart by ever more violent deeds. Doctor Henry's gentle dismay at the events of 1922 is echoed in the dilemma of those who found themselves caught between extremes in the beleaguered Ulster of the 1970s.

5

For the Political Record

Peadar's next volume was an autobiographical one. In 1932 he published *The Gates Flew Open*, which tells the story of his jail experiences after he was made prisoner by the Free State troops on the fall of the Four Courts. This book and especially its sequel, *There Will be Another Day*, which did not appear until 1963, are among the relatively few primary sources for anyone wishing to study the political history of the period. It is a curious fact that while politicians in other countries are scarcely out of office before they are busy at their memoirs—one thinks of Churchill, de Gaulle, Lyndon Johnson and many others—Irish political leaders have been strangely reticent. Many, of course, were cut down before leisure presented itself, as was the case with Collins, Mellows, Kevin O'Higgins. Arthur Griffith died before he could record the climax to his life's campaign. But one might have expected de Valera memoirs, and there are none. O'Donnell was not one of the military leaders on the republican side, nor, because he maintained the abstentionist stand in politics, was he ever active in government. But he was always close to the Republican leadership during the dozen years following the split over the Treaty, and he was certainly the most literate among them, so his testimony has documentary value for the historian.

Peadar was thirty when he first found himself in jail, a little older than most of his fellow-prisoners. His initial reactions were probably no different from those of many a country lad accustomed to the light, the open sky, and the wind, and suddenly deprived of them. *The Gates Flew Open* depicts them:

> When the cell door banged shut with a short thick-set thud, my mind went dark; I felt buried; I was as full of panic as a child, who, searching nervously in the distant corner of a barn at night time, is trapped by a gust of wind which slams the door and puts out the candle; it was as bad as that. I was on the floor, for I had been catapulted in by the jailers, and the darkness was smothering me. Did you ever crouch on a helm when there was no sky and the squalls were heavy with blackness and the roar of surf, and there was no air thin enough to breathe?

But these reactions soon passed.

Jail days are the revolutionary's university in more senses than one. Mountjoy was an old prison, and though prisoners were supposed to be in single cells, quick wits soon put an end to that. A Bible, thoughtfully provided by the authorities, inserted near the hinge when a heavy cell-door was being slammed shut was sufficient to force it out of true and make it impossible to lock again without major repair. A blanket tied

round two window-bars and then slowly twisted tight
with a stick would bend even stout iron. Bricks and
mortar gave way before men accustomed to wrest their
tiny farms from the rocky landscapes of western Ireland.
The prisoners had soon broken a line of communica-
tions from cell to cell and from ward to ward. They
could not, of course, have done these things if their
guards had been resolute, but this was the early nine-
teen-twenties, before the grim ruthlessness of Stalin's
Ogpu or Hitler's Gestapo had cast their shadow on
modern history. In any case, the lines between the two
sides in the civil war were not clearly drawn. Many of
the guards were waverers, ashamed to find themselves
guarding men who had recently shared danger with
them in facing a common enemy. Sympathetic inter-
mediaries among them soon made it possible to establish an efficient courier service with the outside world.
As already mentioned, Lile O'Donel was the outside
contact with the Irregulars still at large.

But jail was a chance to sharpen the mental faculties
as well. Peadar read voraciously all he could lay hands
on—Shakespeare, Dickens, P. G. Wodehouse—and it was
now that he first began seriously to write. Many of the
prisoners too were eager to further their often very
rudimentary education and the old schoolmaster's services were in demand for adult classes. There were long
theoretical discussions with Sean MacBride, Liam Mellows, Dick Barrett, Rory O'Connor, Joe McKelvey. The
last four were all to give their names to bitter legend
at dawn on December 8, 1922, when they were sum-
marily shot in a desperate attempt by the Free State

executive to end the civil war by terror. When O'Donnell was taken from Mountjoy to Finner camp in Donegal to be put in close confinement, it was clear that he was to be held as hostage for the behavior of his brother Frank outside. But that proved a game both sides could play. The Republicans were strong in Donegal and a list of local Free State supporters who would be shot if Peadar O'Donnell was harmed was drawn up and the individuals quietly informed. It cannot be known if this threat, or Lile O'Donel's flamboyant gesture in Dublin was decisive, but at all events Peadar lived to tell the tale.

The Gates Flew Open is not written with the care and skill the author gave to his novels. Often the writing is slangy and slipshod. But it does convey vividly the feel of the times. There was bitter anticlericalism among the prisoners. The great majority of the Irish clergy were denouncing virulently those who took the anti-Treaty side. Some even made physical assaults on the few fellow-clergy who took the minority view. Prison chaplains went to the length of refusing to say the traditional prayers for the dead in the case of known Republicans after the bishops had excommunicated unrepentant adherents of the IRA. "May you be the mother of a bishop!" is a traditional pious greeting among women in Ireland. But in the jails of 1922, O'Donnell tells us, Irish girls hurled it at others as a malediction. Reading these pages, one certainly does not feel that the scene in *The Knife* where the Republicans invade the altar to prevent the priest from preaching politics is in any way exaggerated.

Peadar was twenty-one months in his various jails. While he was in Kilmainham, toward the end of that period, the Republican leadership decided to adopt the tactic of the hunger strike. Under the British, Terence MacSwiney, Lord Mayor of Cork, had fasted to his death after seventy-four days, and world opinion had been successfully focused on the callousness of the jailers who let him die. If it was believed the Free Staters would prove more soft-hearted than the British, this proved an error. A few prisoners were released on condition they abandon the strike and sign parole, but even on this the captors' policy was a capricious one. The strike continued until two men died, when the leadership decided to call it off. Peadar himself was very weak and not far from hospitalization by this time; he too had come dangerously near to the end.

On the eve of St. Patrick's Day, 1924, O'Donnell walked through the gates of the Curragh camp to freedom. Strictly speaking, he had never been a prisoner, only a detainee, since the Free State did not recognize Republicans as prisoners-of-war and he had not been charged with a criminal offense. He was to be arrested from time to time in later years, and in 1926 he spent six weeks on remand awaiting trial for activities in the land annuities agitation. Eventually he was acquitted. It was a deliberate tactic of the Free State police to haul in known Republicans for arbitrary questioning at times when this would create difficulties in their employment or embarrass their private lives. This practice had to be abandoned when its legality was successfully challenged in the courts. The Northern authorities

issued a prohibition on Peadar's entering the North
when he was due to address a meeting at Cave Hill near
Belfast. The meeting was abandoned, though in fact the
prohibition had been served on another Republican in
error.

News that the civil war had ended on May 24, 1923,
had reached Peadar and his comrades in jail. Although
it represented the defeat of the cause they stood for,
the news was greeted—at least by many of the younger
prisoners—with excitement and joy. Because of the
manner in which the war ended there was no question
of releasing the detainees overnight. But there was an
immediate improvement in conditions. Food became
better; books and writing materials were freely obtain-
able; the guards relaxed and were often ready to chat
and do small favors for those they guarded pending
individual decisions on release.

De Valera and the Republican Army in the field had
ended hostilities with the formula Trotsky first devised
at Brest-Litovsk: no war, no peace. The order was to
bury arms and go quietly home, not surrender. In his
famous message to "Soldiers of the Republic, Legion
of the Rearguard," de Valera announced: "The Republic can no longer be defended successfully by your
arms. . . . Military victory must be allowed to rest for
the moment with those who have destroyed the Republic. Other means must be sought to safeguard the
nation's right." The prime reason for the Republicans'
defeat was that the ordinary people—even though they
showed by their votes in 1923 and later, that de Valera's
charisma was still strong—wished for peace. Repeatedly

this century it has been shown that a guerilla movement is almost invincible if it has the hinterland with
it; it is doomed if it has not. Volunteers who found safe
billets in country homes during the war against the
British now found themselves unhappy, hunted men
sleeping out on the hills. De Valera's message admitted
the reality. But implicit was the threat that if more
favorable circumstances offered, the war would be renewed. The Free State government was determined
favorable circumstances would not be offered.

It was accordingly a bewildered, often embittered
populace Peadar found outside the jail gates. Appalling,
unbelievable things had been done in the name of the
national cause. Prisoners had been taken from jail and
shot by simple executive order, sometimes while legal
appeals were unsettled before the courts. Republicans
surrendering in the field had been tortured for information, or tied in groups to landmines, which were
then detonated. The Republican command had retaliated by issuing orders that known public supporters of
the usurping Free State were to be shot at sight. Violence answering violence, in the words of Lady Gregory's private diary, "like the clerks answering at the
mass."

For the more thoughtful leaders of the national
movement, the civil war period presented a nightmare
dilemma. Many ministers of the fledgling Free State
government, men like Cosgrave, Mulcahy, Kevin
O'Higgins, defended their actions in brash, almost flamboyant language in public while confessing their doubts
and soul-searchings in private. Their argument was that

they must do evil things to prevent the worse evil of anarchy throughout the country. Kevin O'Higgins, hated by Republicans for the apparent heartlessness of his words on public occasions, told friends: "a man who has done what I have done, cannot expect to live"—and seems to have accepted death almost thankfully when he was gunned down by political enemies four years after the cease-fire. De Valera, whom many held personally responsible for the events leading to civil war, vacillated at the time and equivocated in his subsequent explanations of his actions. Gavan Duffy, who had signed the Treaty in the hope of salvaging national unity, veered to opposing the Treatyites when he realized the events it had brought in train.

O'Donnell seems to have had no misgivings, either then or later, over the position he upheld: the Treaty was a British-imposed settlement, signed by renegade Irishmen, only upheld by British aid and arms. He had no bitterness toward his opponents. In his view they were mere miserable dupes and place-men—"Seaneens" (little John Bulls) or West Britons. This was probably the general attitude of the Republican leaders. There was more bitterness on the side of the Free Staters, who found that in exercising the unromantic virtue of prudence they were isolating themselves from the mainstream of national sentiment.

The IRA leadership, pledged to continue the struggle until an all-Ireland Republic was achieved, was still intact, and O'Donnell was a member of it. Official IRA doctrine was that it was trustee for the only legitimate government, deriving this claim from the Proclamation of Easter Monday 1916. It was both a military and a patriotic organization, curiously combining a belief in the sovereignty of the Irish nation and a distrust of the majority will of the Irish people. The paradox voiced by Maire MacSwiney, widow of the dead Lord Mayor of Cork, expressed their attitude: "The people have no right to be wrong."

The constitution of the IRA was ingeniously devised to make public and conspiratorial activity equally possible. The controlling body was the army convention, elected from the local units, and electing in its turn an executive committee of twelve. These twelve, meeting under pledge of secrecy, then elected the army council of seven, which formed the executive. The seven need not be from the executive committee. Thus their identity was only divulged to the rank-and-file or to the general public when expediency demanded this. The Chief of Staff, the leader, has usually been familiar to the newspaper-reading public, as have some of his lieutenants. From civil war days until his break with the organization in 1934, O'Donnell was always one of the seven and one of the twelve.

Peadar himself has often stated that his influence within the IRA has been exaggerated owing to the fact that he was the most literate member of the controlling body. For this reason policy statements or resolutions were usually drafted by him and bore the thumbprint of his style. It is hard for an outsider to verify if this reflects false modesty or fact. But he was certainly both vocal and active in the decade following the split. In the first army convention after the civil war, it was

O'Donnell who sponsored the important resolution by which the IRA withdrew allegiance from the civilian Republican Government and declared itself an independent organization. (The almost theological reasoning of Republican diehards was that the civilian government of the country was represented by the *minority* of elected delegates in the Irish parliament who had refused to vote for the Treaty, thereby remaining true to the Proclamation of 1916.)

In the 1920s and the first half of the 1930s Peadar O'Donnell was busily engaged in a variety of activities. The fact that marriage had freed him from the necessity to earn a living meant that he had time to give to revolutionary agitation, which most of his associates lacked. He could also travel. As we have seen, he was producing at this period a steady flow of novels. He had already been editor of *An t'Oglach,* the illegal newssheet of the IRA and in April 1926 he also became editor of the official organ, *An Phoblacht,* which appeared weekly except when it was suppressed or seized by the authorities. This paper had been founded nine months previously under the mantle of Eamon de Valera, whose sponsorship ceased when he decided to enter constitutional politics as leader of the new political party, Fianna Fail, which he himself founded, and to rally his supporters through the daily *Irish Press,* of which his family became the principal shareholders.

The first issue of *An Phoblacht* had contained among other things a signed article by "President de Valera" on the legacy of the Treaty, and an appeal by Maud Gonne MacBride on behalf of the 80 political prisoners

who were still held in Irish, Scottish, and English jails.
Subsequent issues carried articles by Hannah Sheehy
Skeffington, widow of the pacifist Francis Skeffington,
who was shot in 1916; by Peadar himself; and a series
of pieces by Father Michael O'Flanagan, a great and
subtle mob orator and a priest who had been "silenced"
(forbidden to preach) by his ecclesiastical superiors for
his support of the Republican cause. The paper was far
from parochial. There were comments and news about
the exciting events in the young Soviet Russia and in
Chiang Kai-chek's China, both seen at the time as
natural allies in the struggle against the last remnants
of British imperialism.

Under Peadar's editorship an immediate change became apparent. There was still the strident campaign
against the truly appalling conditions in Irish jails and
the brutality of the police, which on more than one
occasion led to prisoners' having to be removed to state
mental hospitals. To turn over the pages of *An Phoblacht* today is to be sickened by the reminder of how
near the surface violence is in every community and
how it will proliferate immediately the civilized veneer
is pushed aside. Physical brutality was not the monop-
oly of one side. Frank Ryan, who was a close friend
and associate of O'Donnell, is on record with "While
we have fists and boots, and guns if need be, we will
not allow free speech to traitors." Peadar himself never
voiced such sentiments, but he made clear that he had
no patience with the principle of "the freedom of the
press." In the issue of 17 December 1926, he asks: "Who

will question the wisdom of shutting down enemy news-
papers in 1916?"

A really new feature was the regular column on
literary topics. This was a paper largely circulating
among working men and we find again the schoolmaster's drive for adult education. Another element was
the emphasis on social and economic questions. The
census of 1926 revealed that emigration from the country was running at 71,000 inhabitants per annum.
Under a headline *Race Extermination,* the paper described the Census Commission's verdict as "the most
terrible that could be laid to the charge of any government."

Almost by chance an issue presented itself that dra-
matically offered the possibility of linking popular agitation for the betterment of the poor with national
struggle against the outside imperial power. This was
the campaign over what were known as the Land Annuities. The story of this agitation is unfolded in the
book Peadar always said he most enjoyed writing, *There
Will be Another Day* (1963).

The legal aspect of the land annuity payments is a
complicated one. The moral aspect could be stated, at
least for propaganda purposes, quite simply in the
words of the French philosopher: "The origin of property is theft." During the British occupation, land had
been seized from the indigenous Irish and distributed,
and often redistributed, among the conquerors, who
came to form what later generations termed the Anglo-
Irish ascendancy. As a result of the land agitation in

the nineteenth century, many of the estates thus established were taken over by the Irish Land Commission,
which was set up by British act of parliament, to be
parceled out as small holdings for landless laborers and
tenant farmers. The former owners were compensated
by Land Bonds. The new occupiers paid a fixed annual
sum under an agreement that eventually the land would
pass to them as freehold. In other words, it was a hire-
purchase agreement or purchase under the installment
plan.

During the fighting of the revolutionary years many
of these small farmers had fallen into arrears over payments, and in the first postwar slump of the early nine-
teen-twenties they found it hard to make the current
payments, let alone compensate for arrears. The terms
of the Treaty with the British were somewhat ambiguous. They certainly provided that the annuities would
still be collected by the Land Commission, now under
control of the Free State. The British claimed, and the
Cosgrave government conceded, that they should then
be handed over to Britain. The total amount was substantial. In a speech in 1934 de Valera was to claim that
it laid a heavier burden on Ireland than war reparations
did on Germany after 1918 and he claimed that in 1931
it almost equaled the total value of Irish cattle exports.

There were also estates that had not yet been ac-
quired by the Land Commission where rents were still
being paid directly to British landlords. It was on one
of these, that of the Marquess of Conyngham in Donegal (Peadar's father's own farm once belonged to this
estate), that trouble started as early as 1919. The official

policy of the national movement, after Connolly's death, had always been that no change should be made in the social system until the enemy was cleared from the country. Then such problems could be discussed; meanwhile the status quo must be upheld. Sinn Fein courts in areas liberated from the British were actually enforcing payments of rents. But there was a more revolutionary temper in parts of Donegal. In this case a local meeting in the village hall decided that landlordism was out, neither rent penny nor land annuity was morally due, and the local IRA commandant, Joe Sweeney, who was once a pupil at St. Enda's, the school founded by the first President of the Irish Republic, Patrick Pearse, sheltered the new policy.

Peadar O'Donnell had no hand in this decision. He was busy fighting elsewhere at the time. In fact he tells us frankly in *There Will be Another Day* that he was very slow to realize the possibilities opened up by this issue. He heard and sympathized with the odd hardship, read of the occasional bailiff's seizure of cattle against nonpayment of rent. Then, in late 1925 or early 1926:

> one day a thing happened. Jack Boyle of Croveigh, a man at whose fireside I had often found welcome and warmth and food, handed me a letter which warned him that unless he paid his arrears of land annuity before a stated date, court proceedings would be taken against him and legal costs would add to his burden. We sat on a flag by the roadside on a sunny day and when, fumbling and awkward, I said maybe it would be a mistake to let the cost of court proceedings overtake him, he told me it just did not matter. The arrears were beyond him. To pay

that sum he would have to sell his few head of cattle. There were others in his plight. If the bailiff came the worst he could do was drive away his few cattle. He went on his way and I sat there, the threatening letter still in my hand. The envelope was distinctive and I called on one of the local postmen and asked him if he had delivered letters of this kind and he had, and he named people to me. I was a native of the district and it was easy for me to wander around and pick up enough to give myself an idea of the state of things, on the level of neigbourly gossip.

I consulted nobody, told nobody of my intention, but on the following Sunday I was on the wall by the chapel gate to make a speech as the people came out from Mass.

That speech was the opening of a campaign to withhold rents and to get together as neighbors to obstruct by every reasonable means the bailiffs who would come after them. There was more than a hint that if the bailiffs proved unreasonable men, there would be no harm in using unreasonable methods either.

Peadar was a born orator, a natural agitator, and this was a theme and a campaign closer to heart and more congenial than skirmishing with the British or debating the niceties of Republic versus Free State. The days that followed were exciting and exhilarating—bicycling into remote townlands, rowing across to visit villages the other side of the bay, organizing the stalwarts, convincing the waverers, maneuvering to pressurize blacklegs who might buy seized cattle. Fine vivid characters stand out from these pages—"tough, mountain folk who live in the Fenian tradition to a pattern of behaviour that has survived among us from far-off days." Here is a story of Black James Duirnin, who went to jail for not paying rent and was presented with £25 collected by a publicity-seeking busybody from the neighbors when he came out:

> Black James thanked the man who handed him the money. He asked him to thank every person who put a red penny into this fine gift and to say that he, himself, thanked them from his heart; it was clear that he was deeply moved. Up went the shaggy old head. "Thank them and give them their money back. I went to jail for a principle. I could have paid the annuity and the arrears."

And Peadar?

> I just looked on, in a flood of tears, feeling a fool and, in my own way, rejoicing I was there to see what I saw.

There could be harrowing incidents too in these visits to simple country people:

> a woman who lost her boy in the fight in defence of the Republic unloaded onto me the bitterness she had hidden from everybody else; by great good luck I called on her by myself so that she got the opportunity. Her boy was working in a field when I went by and he left his work and went with me and was killed. She bolted the door behind me and went on her knees and she cursed me and cursed me and as she cursed, short bursts of words escaped and they told the story. I was very sorry for her. When the storm ended I took her by the hand and helped her to her feet and I scolded her for doing her boy so great a wrong, by making him, in her own mind, a poor fool with no mind of his own, taken by the hand into danger when, in fact, he was a thoughtful, even brilliant man. It was natural she should begrudge him, but she should

not make little of him in her own heart. We drank tea together.

As these passages show, Peadar had one secret weapon to use in his revolutionary activities, which he tells us he learnt from his father and Black James Duirnin. "Their secret? They both liked people."

The campaign snowballed, outward from Donegal until it was nationwide. Without asking for authorization O'Donnell used his editorship of *An Phoblacht* to give it a forum. Some of the IRA executive looked askance at this as side-tracking the national issue, a trespassing into "politics." But clearly the agitation was too popular with the rank-and-file members to be cold-shouldered. Inevitably the Catholic hierarchy fulminated and denounced O'Donnell as a communist. Not every priest followed the hierarchy. Father John Fahy, a curate in Galway, gave vigorous support. Some clergy, incredible as it seems, were proposing that the duty to pay rent should be made part of the child's catechism taught in schools. Father Fahy produced a satirical alternative catechism, which Peadar printed in *An Phoblacht*:

How did England establish a claim to the land of Ireland? By robbery.
What is rent? Rent is a tribute of slavery enforced by the arms of the robber-landlord.
What is a landlord? A landlord is a descendant of a land robber.
Who pay rents to landlords? Only slaves.
What is a bailiff? A bailiff is a land robber's assistant.
What should be done with a bailiff . . . with a landlord?

Another ally, a strange one, was Colonel Maurice Moore, brother of the novelist and a Senator of the Irish Free State. The Moores of Moore Hall in County Mayo were Catholic landlords who had a good reputation in watching over the welfare of their tenants. Their home was shamefully burnt down by unknown Republicans during the troubled times, but Colonel Moore was no way embittered. He called at the O'Donnell home in Dublin one day with the manuscript of a pamphlet, *British Plunder and Irish Blunder,* in which he passionately argued the legal case against handing over the land payments to Britain. Obviously an attack from this quarter would gravely disconcert the government. After a brief hesitation, O'Donnell accepted the ally. Jointly a meeting was planned for Loughrea and publicized by posters under the heading CALL OFF THE BAILIFFS.

Moore was also a useful intermediary with de Valera, whose stand was at first cautious, but who was impressed by the legal arguments, as also by the tactical advantages the campaign offered against the government in office. Agitation over the annuities was strong in de Valera's own constituency in County Clare, one of the poorer western counties. The campaign became part of Fianna Fail's official program and the party went into the 1932 election on a dual platform: remove the oath of allegiance to Britain and withhold the land annuities. It yielded a landslide victory. To the dismay of his followers, the Chief was not anxious to concede their demands in full. Payments were still to be made, but they were to be held in the Irish exchequer and used to relieve general taxation. In the end a compromise was agreed on: annual payments were to be halved, recent arrears funded, older arrears to be overlooked.

The British retaliated against the Irish government's policy of withholding payments by raising a customs barrier against Irish produce's entering England, thus inaugurating what became known as the economic war. Here too eventually a compromise was reached. As part of the Anglo-Irish package settlement of 1938 a lump sum was handed over and the issue of annual payments closed.

Thus ended the most exhilarating period in Peadar O'Donnell's life, a campaign vigorously and joyfully fought in which he was indisputably the principal actor. He had been arrested once in the course of it, and even that provided a colorful occasion he had enjoyed. He followed the traditional Republican policy of refusing to recognize the court. He remained silent, and to his amusement discovered that this put the court to the trouble of deciding whether he was mute "of nature or of malice." When the legal debate was almost ended, he gave the answer quietly himself: "Malice, sheer malice," eliciting reluctant smiles from the jurors, whom he then addressed to explain that he had nothing against them personally, they were countrymen like himself, but he wasn't interested in "the fellow in the wig." He was not convicted.

Notwithstanding, from the strictly revolutionary viewpoint, the outcome of the campaign was failure. Property relationships remained intact, and the hope that refusal to pay rent would be the first step to communal farming had proved premature. But *Another Day* closes with a sanguine hope for a socialist future:

> Fenian Ireland, the Ireland of the poor, came to the very doorstep of a struggle for power twice in ten years; in 1922 and again in 1931. In each case it failed to achieve a leadership to correspond with its needs and was driven back in confusion. It has paid a heavy price in mass emigration for those failures. It has, however, gained sharp, political lessons; the lesson of 1922, even only half-learned, is apparent in the IRA search for a policy in 1931. Other men, in other days, will contemplate those mistakes, for of course the Ireland of the poor will be back. There will be another day.

It remains to be seen whether the 1970s will prove to have written that further chapter in Fenian history.

6

Toward a Socialist Ireland

The preceding chapters have made abundantly clear that Peadar O'Donnell's entire outlook on life, expressed in his work as an agitator and a writer, was that of a man of the left. But the relationship between socialism and nationalism in Ireland is an involved one and calls for some discussion if we are to understand Peadar's position against the evolution of the modern Irish state.

Socialists from the more advanced powers often have difficulty in appreciating the importance attributed to the national struggle by socialists in the emergent nations. But if it is remembered that socialism is the revolt of the underprivileged against the propertied classes, and nationalism that of the underprivileged peoples against the imperialist powers, it is easy to see what the two movements have in common. For Peadar the identification of the two causes was complete. For him the term *republic* had its basic sense, that of a government directly controlled by the ordinary people, not by the wealthy few. In this his thinking was in direct succession to that of James Connolly, who had written: "We cannot conceive of a free Ireland with a subject working-class; we cannot conceive of a subject Ireland with a free working-class."

But for others, this identification was far from valid. Even in Connolly's day, the fiery trade-union leader, Larkin, stood aside from the national struggle; at the opposite end of the political scale Padraic Pearse's mystical ideal of nationhood assigned no special role to the working-class. Connolly himself had been slow to make the synthesis. Just before the Easter Rising of 1916 he attended a secret rendezvous with the leaders of the Irish Republican Brotherhood, at which the whole issue was threshed out. The upshot was that Connolly was co-opted onto the military council, and henceforward embraced with complete conviction the nationalist creed. De Valera's viewpoint was similar to that of Pearse. He believed that "Labour must wait." The essential, he considered, was to rid Ireland of economic servitude to Britain and the last symbols of British rule; then domestic political issues could be discussed. The nationalism of the Free State leaders was even less radical. They wished control of the country to pass from English to Irish hands, but they wished no change in the social structure. Irish capitalism would replace British capitalism. There was, in actual fact, a surprising amount of state and semi-state capitalist enterprise under both Cosgrave and de Valera, but this was due to accidental, not ideological, reasons. Inexperience and distrust felt by Irish entrepreneurs for projects at home made it necessary for the state to provide capital for such schemes as the harnessing of the Shannon for electric power.

Within the IRA itself there were divergent tendencies. On the whole, rank-and-file members came from the underprivileged classes. But the leadership embraced some who shared the view that "Labour must wait" and others who believed that talk of the class struggle was positively disruptive of the class synthesis they held to be the nation. Peadar, of course, fought stubbornly to make the IRA an instrument for socialist revolution and in this he was not alone. He believed that the IRA should be in the forefront of every struggle for the betterment of the workers and small farmers and that as organs of the struggle for freedom they must prepare to transform themselves into the organs of government for the country—in order, as he phrased it, to prevent "a group of twopenny-halfpenny lawyers getting into power by the democratic vote." The nearest parallel to the role he wished the IRA to play was that of the Bolshevik party in Russia under Lenin, and his attitude toward conventional democracy was similar to that of Lenin.

O'Donnell was able, as we have seen, to use his place as editor of *An Phoblacht* to propagandize the struggle over the Land Annuities but he was unable to get the IRA as an organization behind the campaign. In consequence de Valera and Fianna Fail reaped the propaganda victory from the agitation O'Donnell had started. On the IRA executive, once the radicalism of the civil war period had subsided, O'Donnell found himself increasingly outvoted. The Army Convention of 1933, while itself formulating a program of "national reconstruction and establishment of social justice," passed a resolution forbidding volunteers from writing or speaking on social, political, or economic questions. If enforced, this would of course have left no room for a man of O'Donnell's convictions. At the following year's convention, Peadar O'Donnell and George Gilmore proposed a plan for summoning a wide congress of all republican movements in the country; when this was defeated, narrowly and only by the votes of the executive, they withdrew from the convention to call this congress themselves. Frank Ryan accompanied them. Both Gilmore and Ryan were veterans of the war of independence and the civil war who shared Peadar's socialist views.

The new body met at Athlone and called itself the Republican Congress. Popularly it became known as the 'Red IRA' to distinguish it from the older organization, which became the 'Green IRA'. Peadar left his editorship of *An Phoblacht* to become editor of a new weekly, *Republican Congress*. He was court-martialed in his absence by the IRA for these activities. When he heard about this, he remarked that since they had court-martialed him in his absence, any sentence the secret tribunal passed might as well be executed in his absence too.

The urgency to break away from the purely military IRA to form a broader-based movement, which prompted the hiving-off to found the Republican Congress, was the threat of fascism in Ireland. The early

years of the Irish Free State were certainly turbulent
ones, having far more in common with events on the
continent of Europe than with those in Britain. The
waylaying and beating-up of political opponents, or the
odd murder of a police officer, an informer, or an IRA
dissident, hardly made the headlines. In 1926 it looked
as though a second round of the civil war might take
place; a state of emergency was proclaimed. In 1931
military tribunals were revived to deal with political
offenses. Over the whole of this period the form of the
new state was constantly under discussion.

Fascism was not then the dirty word it became after
the Second World War and the defeat of the axis
powers. There were many in Ireland who admired
Mussolini's character and forcefulness, and who felt
that the theory of the corporate state and the practical
educational proposals of the Italian philosopher Gentile
were more fertile prototypes for the new Ireland than
a slavish taking over of British democracy and the man-
darin-style higher education Britain had evolved to provide administrators for a colonial empire. The poet
Yeats, then a Free State Senator, was referring to Mussolini in his speech at the Tailteann Games in Dublin
in 1924 when he said "A great popular leader has announced to an applauding multitude, 'We will trample
on the decomposing body of the goddess of liberty.' "
He went on to end with a subtle reference to Lenin:

> and generations to come will have for their task, not the
> widening of liberty, but recovery from its errors—the
> building up of authority, the restoration of discipline,
> the discovery of a life sufficiently heroic to live without
> the opium dream.

After de Valera had acceded to power, many supporters of the previous government openly questioned the theory of parliamentary democracy. Ernest Blythe, former Minister for Finance, stated: "The Dail is not suitable for modern government. This miscellaneous assembly is not a suitable assembly for discussing the business of the nation." Professor Tierney of University College, Dublin, championed the corporate state as "a scheme of social and political organization which is quite certain as time goes on to be adapted to the needs of every civilized country." The Papal encyclical of 1931, *Quadragesimo anno,* which spoke of vocational organization as the basis of "true and genuine social order," inevitably had an attentive hearing in Ireland. As late as 1939 the de Valera government appointed an official commission to enquire into the idea of vocational organization and economic democracy under Irish conditions. It reported, somewhat inconclusively, in 1943 and nothing whatever was done about its recommendations.

In the early 1930s, in consequence of these trends, a definite fascist movement arose in Ireland. Although it progressed through various names, it has gone down in history as the Blueshirt movement. Its forerunner was the Army Comrades Association, formed by government supporters in 1931 primarily with a view to preventing their meetings from being broken up by IRA or left-wing hecklers. After de Valera's electoral victory, the Free State government conceded power peacefully, but immediately afterwards the Army Comrades Association became a rallying point for those unreconciled to defeat, and it mushroomed out along regular fascist lines, adopting the Blue shirt, black tie, and black beret as uniform and assuming the Roman fascist salute of raised arm and open palm. General O'Duffy, a civil war veteran from the Free State side, who had been dismissed by de Valera from his post as chief of police, became the leader. Mulcahy, Blythe, Dillon, Costello, and others supported the movement, sometimes voicing their admiration for the continental dictators in terms that would later seem surprising. On 10 August 1933, a mass parade of Blueshirts was announced, to assemble outside the parliament and government buildings in Dublin. Special trains were chartered to bring supporters up from the country. It looked extremely like an attempt to emulate Mussolini's successful march on Rome of 1922. But the de Valera government reacted vigorously. The parade was banned, the army mobilized to enforce the ban. At the same time the power to operate military tribunals, the very power that the Free State government had inserted in the constitution mainly against de Valera's followers, was evoked to uphold the security of the state. O'Duffy dropped the challenge and called the parade off. The movement gradually disintegrated and became absorbed into the new parliamentary opposition party, Fine Gael, of which O'Duffy was for a short while leader.

The reasons why fascism triumphed in Italy and Germany and, after a full-scale civil war, in Spain, while failing, in spite of initial promise, in countries like France and Ireland are matters of conjecture for the historian. But undoubtedly one factor in Ireland was that de Valera, unlike the pre-fascist premiers in Italy and Germany, was resourceful and determined. Perhaps from his revolutionary background, perhaps from his study of Machiavelli's teaching while he was in British jails, he had short hesitation in utilizing undemocratic measures in order to uphold democratic freedom. Later, he used the military tribunals to protect his government from the menace of his earlier associates, the IRA.

It is easy to be wise after the event, but the threat of fascism in Ireland seemed a real one in the 1930s. Peadar O'Donnell opposed it with the instinct of a radical who had not lost touch with the working-class movement, not that of an intellectual who might have felt the pull of certain elements in the new ideology. As far as Peadar was concerned, he saw that the leaders of the Blueshirt movement were the rancher interests in the countryside, the gombeen men in the small towns, the well-to-do classes of the cities, and their hangers-on—and he was against them. His was the classical view of the European communists that fascism represented the final gamble of capitalist imperialism. The only way to counteract the new demagogy, which might erode the support of waverers in the laboring classes, was to organize an alternative mass movement, which must be based in Ireland on the mountainy farmers and farm-laborers, the wage-earners in the towns, and the unemployed, whose numbers were being swelled by the great economic slump. That was the view behind the walk-out from the IRA to form the Republican Congress.

Even inside the Congress, however, a fresh division of opinion immediately appeared. There was a small, but vocal, communist movement in Ireland. Peadar had had a hand in the founding in 1930 of the Workers' Revolutionary Party of Ireland, with Sean Murray, from one of the small farms of Antrim, as secretary. Peadar does not seem to have been a party member. In fact he took a somewhat ill-advised libel action against a Catholic paper that claimed he was. Yeats was invited to give evidence on this occasion on Peadar's behalf and according to the press reports delivered his opinion that he "wished this young man would confine himself to literature and leave politics to his old age." However that might be, Peadar's distinctive style was evident in some issues of the party organ, *The Workers' Voice*. At that time the communists all over Europe were divided over what allies they would accept in the fight against fascism. Before the accession of Hitler, the German communists had spent more energy dividing the socialist movement than in oposing the Nazis, but after 1933 the line changed. Followers of the communist international everywhere favored a united front with socialists, liberals, and anyone else sincerely opposed to Hitlerism, so that in Britain communists even campaigned for Churchill, then an outside conservative, to head a crusade to oust the Chamberlainite appeasers. In the columns of the Irish *Republican Congress* the issue was threshed out in its national and international aspects. Peadar's voice was for the wider front, but its exact borders were hard to draw. Logic would have led to support for de Valera, but this was anathema to the old IRA men who could not forgive him for taking the oath and entering the Free State parliament.

The Republican Congress did not last. After a year it ceased to meet and the paper suspended publication. Peadar O'Donnell continued to be active as an agitator and propagandist, but that was the end of his involvment with organizational politics.

Two of O'Donnell's books, *On the Edge of the Stream* and *Salud!* are written against the background of these times, but before we consider them in the next chapter, we must examine one more facet of Irish life in the fifteen years following independence, and that is the role of the church. Once again we shall find Peadar O'Donnell involved as a controversial figure.

Traditionally the Roman Church in Ireland, at least in modern times, has been regarded as the ally of the Catholic Irish in their struggle against Protestant or agnostic British imperialism. (A medieval Papal bull gave spiritual sanction to English rule in Ireland.) But it was an alliance with strict qualifications. In the early stages of the fight for freedom, many higher clergy were extremely reluctant to endorse what could be construed as an armed rebellion against legally constituted authority. There was also the traditional ban on membership of secret societies. At a later stage they came to support enthusiastically the Free State government, even to the extent of forbidding the sacraments to de Valera's followers in the civil war. At an indeterminate date the excommunication of the defeated Republicans seems to have lapsed and de Valera moved back into grace. But at no stage was the clerical orthodoxy prepared to come to terms, even spiritually, with the irreconcilables in the IRA.

Side by side with anti-Republicanism went anti-communism. Looking back, it is difficult to understand the
basis of the hysterical anti-communism voiced by the
higher and middle clergy and their followers at this
period. Not one of the objective factors that precipi-
tated the Bolshevik revolution in Russia was present
in Ireland. The agrarian question was largely settled
by the Land Acts of the 1890s. There was no large army
of war-weary soldiers and sailors. There were no real
concentrations of underpaid factory workers. Nor was
there much parallel with conditions in Spain, where
the Church owned vast wealth and allied itself with
other large property owners. Red scares, of course, were
a feature of the American scene in both the 1920s and
the 1950s, but these related first to trade-union radicalism, and then to fear of Russia. Neither circumstance
applied to Ireland. The only explanation seems to be
that many of even the higher clergy came from quite
simple homes and found themselves uncertainly admitted to a more-or-less affluent middle class. They became hysterical over what they felt might one day
threaten their new social status.

But anti-communism there certainly was, and it was
usually equated with anti-Republicanism. Peadar, of
course, openly championed both causes, so he was a
sitting target. In 1931 Professor James Hogan of Cork
published a booklet called *Could Ireland become Communist? The Facts of the Case* and devoted most of it
to attacking Peadar personally. It is a good specimen of
the type of argument put forward at the time. In spite
of all, Peadar had many personal friends among the

clergy with whom he was on easy, joking terms, just as he had among the Orangemen of the North.

Oddly enough, none of O'Donnell's books fell afoul of the Irish Censorship Board. Contrary to what is often supposed, this body never had power to ban on either political or theological grounds. Its sole concern was with public morals, which were so interpreted that the only books that met the blue pencil were works advocating contraception or novels dealing frankly or pornographically with sexual activities. Because of his generally extrovert approach as a novelist, Peadar's subject matter escaped the net, though many of his opponents would gladly have put out of bounds the hard anti-clericalism of *The Knife*.

7

Wars in Achill and Spain

It is never easy to combine the life of writer with that of politician, and for a man of Peadar O'Donnell's genial and gregarious temperament it must have been especially difficult. The small house in Drumcondra Road had soon become the Dublin equivalent of the "visiting house" of the Irish countryside—a house where at any time neighbor, former comrade-in-arms, anyone with, or even without, the most casual introduction might lift the latch and open the door, sure of finding a few hours welcome by the fire, and likely as not, if needed, a bed of sorts for the night. In search of a little more quiet time in which to allow Peadar to get on with writing, the O'Donnells began around 1932 to spend a part of each year on Achill Island, County Mayo.

Achill is one of the larger islands off the west coast of Ireland. It is connected by a short bridge with the mainland and is about fifteen miles across. It is relatively thickly populated, the houses clustered in star-shaped villages from which little roads radiate out into the bog and mountain pastures, instead of being built on the strip farms formed in other parts when the big landlords' estates were divided by the Land Commission. The land of Achill in fact was too poor ever to have formed part of a real demesne.

The Achill people have a tough, independent tradition—Peadar has described them as "the freest people in the country," which coming from a Donegal man is a strong compliment. There may be something in the fact, too, that in Cromwellian times the mere Irish were not permitted to live on the islands or within one mile of the coast, though this was not always enforced, so the breed was crossed, just as it undoubtedly was on the fringe of the Ulster plantation. At any rate, Achill Island has a tradition of early marriages and business enterprise that is quite foreign to the inland parts of Mayo and gives it much in common with Donegal.

Peadar was no stranger to Achill. In his days as organizer for the agricultural workers he had frequently stayed and addressed meetings of the potato harvesters migrating from there. Among his friends from former days was a local fisherman, Pat McHugh, and it was in his house that the O'Donnell's rented lodgings. McHugh was actually a pensioner from the pre-independence Dublin Metropolitan Police. That had been a job like many another and did not necessarily make him a supporter of the British connection: he had in fact close sympathies with Connolly's Citizen Army, of which one son later became a member. The McHugh's house stands in the partly Irish-speaking village of the

Bull's Mouth, facing the sound between the island and the mainland. Presumably the name comes from the roar of the tide-race that flows in this narrow sound.

"A man of very great compassion" was how Pat Mc-Hugh's son Michael, who had been a youngster in the 1930s, remembered Peadar. He was thinking particularly of an occasion when a local family was stricken with scarlatina and in consequence shunned by the terrified neighbours. Lile O'Donnell, had, it is true, once run a nursing-home—but only for wounded soldiers. Anyway, both O'Donnells went every day not only to tend the sick but to see to the household chores. Michael McHugh also remembered gratefully Peadar's generosity in giving him the freedom of the small library he had brought with him. Michael read every item from cover to cover.

Achill days for Peadar combined work with play. Breakfast around 9, then writing engrossed at the table with its view over the changing sea and sky, until suddenly the pen would be thrown aside with a shout: "Are ye going fishing today?" In the evening, often the local pub with the neighboring men. Peadar, who never drank and never disapproved of drinking, would sit on the counter and join the fun—"Ye can buy the drinks, lads, and if there's any tay to be bought after, I'll buy the tay."

Peadar went to Achill with a not fully defined intention of writing another novel of rural life. The novel he actually wrote drew at least part of its inspiration from a local agitation in which he was both involved and not involved, since although he was its object, the fact that he was in Achill as a stranger from Donegal gave him what he described as a ringside seat as an observer to study local reactions.

Mention has been made in the last chapter of the virulence with which so many of the Irish clergy at this time were castigating Republicanism, communism, and what they regarded as profligacy in sexual behavior. There was a particularly ferocious parish priest on Achill, Father Campbell, whose zeal embarrassed even some of his most devout parishioners. Patrolling the side roads with a blackthorn to hunt out courting couples was nothing new, but Father Campbell would accost even visiting female tourists who were wearing shorts to tell them the Devil prompted them to wear such indecent clothing. On another occasion at mass, after a blood-and-thunder sermon, he seized the crucifix from the altar and commanded the faithful down on their knees to swear by it that they would have nothing to do with the IRA. Half-a-dozen stalwarts held their ground. It was inevitable that news of Peadar O'Donnell's intended residence should arouse his ire. Though he did not call himself, he sent an emissary to the McHugh household to dissuade them from letting a room to "that Communist." The answer he got from Pat McHugh was: "Let the Devil come out of hell to lodge here, so long as he pays the rent." In this, McHugh was less motivated by anti-clerical defiance than by kin connections, which are never forgotten in rural Ireland, with the O'Donnells. Branches of both families had come from Donegal to settle near Achill and Belmullet a century or two earlier. Subsequently Father Campbell preached a violent sermon against the well-known Red agitator, Peadar O'Donnell, recommending that the local people take the law into their own hands and run him out of the island. Peadar was well able to fight back. The Cosgraveite shopkeepers were against him, but he had the support of some of the tougher local families, who knew that clerical intervention in politics had invariably been hostile to the poorer classes. The agitation was unsuccessful and Peadar left the island when he chose.

Once again, in writing what was to prove his longest novel, *On the Edge of the Stream* (1934), which took him two years to write, Peadar took his observation of the mechanism of local events out of their actual setting and placed them in the Donegal Rosses, where he could use characters and dialogue that flowed naturally from his pen. One Donegal source does enter into this book. Around 1900, a neighbor of the O'Donnells, Patrick Gallagher, had founded in the teeth of bitter opposition from the local merchants the Templecrone Co-operative Society. Peadar knew the details well, even before "Paddy the Cope" set them down in one of the liveliest books of autobiographical reminiscences of rural Ireland, *My Story*.

The opening of *On the Edge of the Stream* sets the scene:

> Derrymore was a Townland that had a lot of its life on view on the road-side—dogs, donkeys, hens, geese, cattle, children; especially children. The houses were so close together that the same noise, and that not a great clamour, could draw heads out of half a dozen doorways.

Derrymore was a local concentration of houses outside the village of Carrick, never referred to by the local people as anything but The Town. But everything is relative, particularly in Ireland, and further into the mountains there were remoter hamlets where Derrymore itself was regarded as a foreign country:

> They had a saying in the townlands beyond that a woman might as well go to America as marry into Derrymore, so little would she visit back among her own folk afterwards.

The first couple of pages in the book also broach the theme. Nelly McFadden has been matched by her mother's scheming with the local priest to the pushing school principal, Ned Joyce. The day she married, her childhood sweetheart Phil Timony up and went to Scotland. The years have passed and now his old mother is sick. A shilling has been found for a telegram to bring the prodigal son home.

He arrives, a corduroy tramp. And shocks the townland shortly after by announcing casually that he has "got out of the habit of going to Mass." But he is a natural worker—even if he passed scalliwag years in Scotland—and a great neighbor. When a local cooperative store is mooted, it seems inevitable that he should step forward to lead it.

The founding of the cooperative has taken place by a half-comic accident. The son of the local merchant house, the Garveys, has just qualified as an attorney and returned to practice in The Town. To celebrate this great occasion—and no doubt with an eye to future business—the Garveys give a party. By some oversight the local doctor, whose son happens to be home from the seminary as a half-fledged priest, is slighted, and in the excitement he calls for a protest meeting. Before anyone quite realizes, the clerical student is called on to make a speech. The only theme he can think of is a talk he recently gave in the seminary on the primitive communism of the early Church. This is seized on eagerly as an attack on the local rich traders—and the game is on. The "Cope" store is founded and the merchants are ready to go to any lengths to smash it. A hellfire sermon from the parish priest falls short; a prayer procession to the house of Phil Timony is accidentally scattered by an excited bull; in the denouement a mission of the Holy Fathers arouses a mob to smash the coop store, but their energies are artfully sidetracked and they wreck the Garveys' premises instead.

There is certainly a large element of farce in all this, which may not be to everybody's taste. Perhaps O'Donnell is here succumbing to a peculiarly Irish weakness. The book still witnesses the keen eye for country life, the same keen ear for a vivid turn of phrase, but it is adulterated by the imposition of knockabout comedy from the outside. This is the convention of juxtaposing realism and serious purpose with farce that O'Casey first introduced to the Abbey Theatre, which then became general in its repertoire, and later appeared in Brendan Behan. Regarded as a propaganda weapon, however, the lighthearted laughter of this book may seem as legitimate a means to expose the merchant-clerical-professional class conspiracy to keep down the poor as the more somber politics of *The Knife.* Satire by farce has a respectable ancestry in the comedies of Molière in France. At any rate, the ranks drawn up for battle in *The Knife* and in *On the Edge of the Stream* are the same.

There is plenty of evidence that what seem farcical crudities in the representation of the merchants' determination to smash the cooperative were not exageration. In *My Story* Paddy the Cope tells how at one point he was solemnly arraigned to be tried under an act of King Edward III as a disturber of the peace for his activities in promoting the cause. He cheerfully went to jail rather than be bound over to silence or accept bail—and returned in triumph three days later freed by intervention from Dublin Castle. In the 1930s prayer processions to ostracize and frighten left-wing agitators alternated with more sinister acts of intimidation against persons and property. In the book Ned Joyce enthuses over the results of a Holy Fathers mission in Dublin:

> A Missioner in Dublin in two nights had the people out wrecking socialist houses. Let us get him down here, and give him a fortnight, longer if he likes.

In 1932 a left-wing headquarters in Eccles Street was gutted by a priests' mob, while the Dublin police made no attempt to intervene. It was not an isolated incident. American readers who recall the witch-hunts of the Father Coughlin era in the States will understand the hysteria that anti-communism can produce.

Miniature wars in Achill and Dublin were but desultory rumblings by comparison with a cataclysmic event soon to take place elsewhere. In the summer of 1936 major civil war erupted in Spain. This terrible blood-letting, worse in relation to population than anything known in western Europe for over a century, had deep repercussions throughout the international scene, and not least in Ireland.

Purely by chance, Peadar was in Catalonia when the war started. Once more he had gone looking for a quiet cottage in a fishing village where he could work undisturbed on a fresh book, and once more lively events caught up with him. His first intention had been to go to Scotland, but his wife and some friends wanted a holiday in Spain and he decided that fisherfolk were much the same everywhere to a man brought up within sound of the sea, so he went too. When his friends returned home, Peadar and Lile settled down for the rest of the summer in a little seaside village thirty miles from Barcelona. The book he intended to write was perhaps *The Big Windows,* but this was soon put on the long finger to be preceded by a hastily composed, but exceedingly vivid account of the Spanish war experience, *Salud! An Irishman in Spain* (1937).

O'Donnell had the advantage over the many foreigners who recorded the Spanish scene at the time that he could compare it with what had happened in Ireland only fifteen years previously. Much of what was taking place had for him "the weird familiarity of a dream." There was the same generous idealism of simple folk caught up in great events, the same spontaneous self-organization, the same enthusiasm leading also sometimes to excesses. In the relationship between the anarchist militia and the loyalist government, once the fighting was underway, he saw an echo of the tug-of-war in Ireland between the IRA and the Republican government. The military men instinctively distrusted the politicians, whom they felt had betrayed them before and would do so again. But they needed them to inform the public and to organize international support. O'Donnell's account of the in-fighting on the loyalist side lacks the political perspicacity of Orwell's *Homage to Catalonia* or Borkenau's *The Spanish Cockpit,* which appeared around the same date. Orwell and Borkenau realized early the sinister maneuvering of the Communist International to suppress grass-root organization in favor of a tight Stalinist-style leadership. The small Spanish communist party was using its control over incoming Russian armaments to strengthen this hold. Where O'Donnell's account gains is in the novelist's intuition of how collective emotion operates. In Barcelona the revolt started at 4 A.M. when Franco's officers ordered their troops from barracks to seize what they hoped would be a sleeping city. But they met their match. This is how O'Donnell describes it:

Who was it first saw and shouted? Some bothered soul, restless that the night watch had been abandoned? Some old body without the strength to keep a strong grip on sleep? A fidgety mother with an ear sharpened to catch the patter of little lives breathing? Anyway, there was a shout. A room leaped to life and roared. A house leaped to life and roared. A street leaped to life and roared. No speeches, for men and women looked and knew, saw and struck. An avalanche of life. Whole families swept into

the bare brightness of the sun, challenging its flash with
the bare brightness of their flesh. "Barricades." There
come moments when all language explodes in dust and
leaves alive only one word which fills the whole of life.
Barricades. Barricades. Furniture leaped into the street—
furniture? Homes came crashing onto the pavement.
Somebody fired a shot.

This suggests the power of an eye-witness account, but
in fact it is a reconstruction, because the O'Donnells
were still in their little fishing village, where the
counter-revolution had not yet struck. He gives an account of how the news was received when it did come,
and of how local committees of anarchists took control of the countryside. The agrarian side of the revolution was of special interest to him. Foreigners could
travel pretty freely in these early days and he saw how
the pattern varied from district to district. In some the
land was seized for immediate dividing into individual
peasant holdings; in others there was an attempt at
cooperative farming. Where the owners of large estates
had fled, indicating clearly where their sympathies lay,
lands were taken over by expropriation. Where the
owners remained, policy varied; often a negotiated
compromise was reached.

O'Donnell makes no attempt to minimize the church-
burnings that took place. This was a curious contrast
to Ireland during the civil war, where although the
clergy were known to be unscrupulously meddling in
politics in favor of the propertied classes, almost no
acts of personal assault or desecration took place. Even
as a foreigner, O'Donnell did not hesitate to denounce
excesses of anti-religious zeal that infringed personal

liberty. At the Customs' barrier outside Barcelona he witnessed a militiaman snatch a crucifix from a twelve-year-old girl and toss it in the air. O'Donnell caught it and loudly demanded of all the militiamen present whether the Anarchist Federation guaranteed freedom of conscience or not. After some sheepish embarrassment, he won his point. It was typical of O'Donnell that when this miniature drama was over, he returned to collect the Customs' man and take him to a café for a friendly chat.

Eager as ever for new experience of human nature, Peadar records visits to both the new men in power in Barcelona and Madrid and those unfortunates not actively engaged on the Franco side who now found their old class-privileges gone. In 1937, just after the Franco forces were first checked outside Madrid, Peadar returned to Ireland.

He found the country gripped in a new wave of anti-communist hysteria. The daily press teemed with atrocity stories of burning churches, ravished nuns, crucified priests. Certainly deplorable incidents had taken, and were to take place. But they were wildly exaggerated. And what they had to do with Ireland was never really clear. Traditionally the Church had been the ally of the common people of Ireland in their days of need, and though politically conscious Republicans resented their stand on the side of the propertied classes in 1922–23, no baptized Irish Catholic would have acted as the Spanish Customs' man had done. Perhaps a British Auxiliary or a Belfast Protestant could. How wealthy the Irish Church is has always been a mystery.

Priests were conspicuous for never traveling second class on the cross channel boat to Britain and nuns attending the national University of Ireland arrived in chauffeur-driven Rolls-Royces, but land—the crux of the property-issue in Ireland, as in Spain—was rarely held by the Church.

O'Duffy's Blueshirts were no longer in the political running. The new rightwing grouping was the Irish Christian Front, led by a wealthy Dublin farmer, Paddy Belton. Mass meetings were held under the slogan: "It is Spain today, it will be Ireland tomorrow." It took courage to champion the cause of the elected government of Spain, threatened with overthrow by army officers commanding Moroccan troops. Irish Republicans realized that the leaders of the Christian Front were their old enemies, the propertied and rancher interests, but they half-believed the shrill propaganda about godless Spanish anarchists and were bewildered by it. Peadar did what he could to present a more realistic picture. Small meetings were held, though on one occasion the crowd was so menacing that Peadar had to climb a lamp-post to address them from there. The Basque nationalists were both fervently Catholic and anti-Franco, which was a useful weapon. Father Laborda, a Basque priest, came to Dublin and spoke alongside O'Donnell and the old Republican priest, Father Michael Flanagan. The real lead against the pro-Franco propaganda in Ireland, however, came from Harry Midgley, the Belfast Labour M.P., who followed the lead of the working-class movement in Britain and France in opposing international Fascism. Even he was

threatened with loss of support among the Catholic
electors, but in a fighting speech he announced that he
would never sell his birthright of liberty for his seat in
parliament.

General O'Duffy was not completely inactive. Having
lost the political limelight to Paddy Belton, he announced that he would lead a contingent of young
Catholic Irishmen to fight against the Reds in Spain.
In fact, about one thousand did enlist, but they saw no
action against the loyalists: their only losses were a result of being fired on by Franco's troops, who mistook
them for the communist-led International Brigade.

Many Irish Republicans, seeing the fascist element in
Ireland so enthusiastic in Franco's support, were determined to take an active part in opposing him. An
Irish unit for the International Brigade was organized,
and it enlisted around two hundred men. It was felt
that either O'Donnell, George Gilmore, or Frank Ryan
should lead it. Gilmore was first choice, but broke a
leg at the critical moment. Frank Ryan was eager to
take his place and went. O'Donnell was not altogether
keen on this venture. He believed that Irish revolutionaries should remain in readiness to take up the fight
again in their own country. But he realized the practical
value for young men of military experience abroad, so,
while he would not actively recruit, he would not dis-
courage those who were determined to go. Young
Michael McHugh, Peadar's Achill friend, tells how he
wished to go and pestered Peadar to tell him how to
do so. In the end Peadar gave him the address of the
International Brigade's recruiting officer in Manchester,

who proved strangely unhelpful. Years after, McHugh learnt that Peadar had written simultaneously to tell the officer not to recruit the young Irishman.

The Spanish war moved to its end in the early summer of 1939. The general European war commenced later the same year. Ireland declared her neutrality, as she was constitutionally entitled to. The vast majority of Irish people supported this. Even those large numbers who joined the British forces often felt that they were doing so to preserve the homeland's peace. There were some in the Republican movement, notably Sean Russell, who believed in the traditional saying: "England's difficulty is Ireland's opportunity." Russell went to Germany, hoping to get Nazi assistance for the unification of Ireland. He obtained a little support, about as much as Casement did in the previous war, and was on his way to Ireland with Frank Ryan in a German submarine when he died suddenly of food poisoning or appendicitis. So strict was inter-sect IRA secrecy that Russell had divulged neither his plans nor his contacts to Ryan. Ryan chose to ask the captain of the vessel to return him to Germany.

Peadar had, of course, by this time no organizational links with the IRA. In general he supported Irish neutrality in the war, but with the proviso that if England were invaded, "Irishmen should fight like terriers beside the British" to drive the Nazis back. He could see no reason for Irishmen to fight in Egypt or Burma.

8

Man of Letters: Editing The Bell; Last Campaigns

Peadar O'Donnell made one contribution in the theatrical field. *Wrack,* a play in six scenes, was first produced by Lennox Robinson at the Abbey Theatre in Dublin on Monday 21 October 1932. It ran for one week. It had one revival in 1935, also for one week.

This play, which made half the night's fare at the theatre, is set on an island off the coast of Donegal, where money is short, men are hungry, and life hard— the background the author knows so well. Herring are sighted at long last, and the boats go out. A storm comes. Most of the boats straggle home, but two are lost and all hands with them. The play ends with the islandwomen keening their dead.

Inevitably one compares this little drama with Synge's *Riders to the Sea,* and the comparison is not pointless because it brings out the difference between the two writers' approach. Synge's drama has the inevit-

ability of Greek tragedy. Its fatalism seems to reflect a
once widespread belief in western Ireland that from
time to time the sea claims a victim and no human
intervention can forestall it. In O'Donnell's approach
there is a hint, certainly not overstressed, of social protest: bigger boats would make the fishing safer, but the
islanders are too poor to afford them. Neighborly soli-
darity is also underscored—Peter Dan, the strongest
fisherman, is lost trying to assist an old comrade's boat
in distress.

It is a stark, moving little story, and tragically true
to life. In the great Atlantic storm of 1928 many west-
of-Ireland fishermen lost their lives, driven by poverty
to tempt a danger they knew, because it was their only
sight of herring in a long, lean spell. But it would be
difficult to claim *Wrack* as a great play. One scene,
that of the storm at sea, takes place on an almost totally
darkened stage. We hear the voices of the fishermen as
they call to each other, and the splash of oars; the only
things seen are the glow of a storm-lantern and the
white catspaw of the foul churning over the stern of
the boat. This scene was rewritten for the second production, but it remains an extremely difficult one to
put across on the stage. The play was published in a
limited edition by Cape in 1933, printing what is presumably the first acted version.

The first night was well attended and well received
—though Peadar liked to attribute this warmth to the
fact that a horse named "Wrack" had just won at the
stakes and members of the racing fraternity had decided
to come to the theatre to celebrate their fancy's prowess!

Press notices describe the author's appearing after "eager applause" to say: "I just wanted to draw aside a window-curtain in a cottage on an island." The *Irish Press* for the following day summed up the general impression:

> (The) play has little plot, slight action and no challenging thought: it is not shaped in accordance with dramatic formulae; it shows inexperience of the stage. But how it charmed and held and moved its audience! How good it was to see in the theatre something so true to nature and to Ireland, so filled with a sense of the humour and pride and pity of human life! . . . Such a play could only be the work of a writer with a passionate knowledge of the life about which he writes.

Some time in the 1950s or 60s O'Donnell submitted a further script, dealing with social problems, to the Abbey directors, but it was considered unsuitable for stage production.

O'Donnell was a founder member of the Irish Academy of Letters, which was founded in 1932 by Yeats and Shaw. The aims of this body at the time of inception can be summarized as twofold: to encourage young writers in need of public recognition and to help old writers in want by making small monetary awards, as circumstances permitted, which it was hoped would attach a cachet and stimulate sales; and to combat the growing monster of state censorship over imaginative literature, which has been referred to earlier in this book. Under Yeats's vigorous guidance it was relatively successful in the first of these aims. Various American and Irish patrons were found to contribute funds for prizes, and medals were struck to honor Irish writers of distinction. Censorship proved a tougher nut to crack and continued to make the land of saints and scholars something of a laughing-stock in the intellectual world until it was substantially modified in the 1950s. The Academy itself became dormant, but did not die, when Yeats passed from the scene in 1939.

Peadar attended Academy meetings reasonably regularly throughout. At the annual general meeting of 1940 he made what seems the rather odd suggestion that the Academy should interest itself in politics. He believed that this would heighten public interest in its existence, and he suggested that it should explore means for raising funds for the dependents of IRA men interned during the "emergency," as neutral Ireland officially described the Second World War. The principle of O'Donnell's proposal was rejected by the meeting, but with Sean O'Faolain's support it was agreed to organize one concert for the charitable purpose suggested.

In August 1958, Peadar became Honorary Secretary to the Academy of Irish Letters, and he held the post until November 1964, when the minutes record that he resigned on account of ill health and was succeeded by Francis Stuart. Both before and after taking office, Peadar's attempts to divert the Academy to a more active role seem to have met frustration. This was partly due to the small membership attending meetings—many Irish writers lived abroad and could not attend, or were elderly and could not attend from ill health, so that it was rare for more than half-a-dozen to turn up to meetings—and partly to lack of funds for awards now that Yeats's contacts and prestige could not be drawn upon. A Council minute of 21 April 1952 records rather sadly:

> Mr O'Donnell suggested that the Academy of Letters should do some work and not remain inactive. Mr Robinson and Mr Mayne were inclined to agree, however, discussion on what work the Academy should do was postponed until a later date.

Elsewhere Peadar complained of "an air of make-believe" current about the Academy's activities.

In any case, the main focus of intellectual life in Ireland during the war years and the decade after was the monthly periodical *The Bell,* from which this last reference is culled. *The Bell* was founded in 1940, with Sean O'Faolain as literary editior and Peadar O'Donnell, though his name does not appear as such, acting as managing editor. After the first six years, O'Faolain withdrew to concentrate on his personal work and Peadar O'Donnell assumed the full responsibility, which he retained until the paper folded in December 1954. For a period Anthony Cronin, who was a frequent contributor to later issues, appeared on the title page as Associate Editor, and it would appear that during Peadar's absences from Dublin he acted as full editor. Around three thousand of each issue were printed, of which one thousand sold outside Ireland.

The Bell has no close counterparts among the cultural magazines of the older-established nations. To understand what it was attempting to do and the problems it faced, it must be remembered that Ireland felt itself to be a young country that had achieved a precarious independence, only eighteen years old, from Britain after many centuries of political, and to a large extent cultural, subjection. A sense of roots is essential to all serious writing and this is what the editors and those round them felt lacking and sought to establish.

When the idea of the paper was first mooted, Bernard Shaw advised O'Faolain to put it in the hands of the established Irish writers and leave them to fill its pages. That might have produced a better literary anthology, but it would not have filled the social and cultural role the editors wished. In the opening editorial, O'Faolain set out:

> THE BELL has, in the usual sense of the word, no policy. We leave it to nature to give the magazine its own time-created character. A boy grows in personality. A man is worth calling a man only in so far as he defines his own character for himself. . . . This is not so much a magazine as a bit of Life itself, and we believe in Life, and leave Life to shape us after her own image and likeness.

He goes on to explain the choice of name:

> THE BELL. Any other equally spare and hard and simple word would have done; any word with a minimum of associations.

Harps and shamrocks had once been symbols of sentimental Irish nationalism, and now Roisin Dubh, Cathleen ni Houlihan and the rest, emblems of the Celtic Twilight, had joined them, cloyed with literary romanticism:

> These belong to the time when we growled in defeat and dreamed of the future. That future has arrived and, with its arrival, killed them. All our symbols have to be created afresh, and the only way to create a living symbol is to take a naked thing and clothe it with new life, new association, new meaning, with all the vigour of the life we live in the Here and Now. . . . All over Ireland—this is the expression of our Faith—there are men and women with things itching them like a grain stuck in a tooth. You who read this know intimately some corner of life that nobody else can know. . . . You know a turn of the road, an old gateway somewhere, a well-field, a street-corner, a wood, a handful of quiet life, a triangle of sea and rock, something that means Ireland to you. . . . These are the things that come at night to tear at an exile's heart. These are the true symbols.

Peadar would have expressed himself in different terminology, just as the jargon of a later generation might have termed this the existentialist approach to editing, but the intention is clear, and on the whole the magazine lived up to it well. The paper must stand for facts and for life, O'Faolain insisted in his third editorial, even at the expense of elegance, if the struggle for cultural identity was to be won.

Thus the paper published a much wider range of material than the conventional literary or political review; it was a ragbag that included poems and other imaginative work from older and younger writers, current reviews of books and plays, reportage on Irish life, and a stream of editorials that some may feel reflect a chip-on-the-shoulder nationalism, or even parochialism, but which could not be avoided in the background of the times. Relations between O'Donnell and O'Faolain were consistently good—both writers have attested this in public—though when O'Donnell took over completely, the political side, as might be expected, became rather more pronounced.

It was not easy to fill the magazine, particularly under the initial conditions of wartime when postal delays and censorship on the part of the belligerent nations made it virtually impossible to get contributions from Irish writers abroad. The editors issued repeated appeals for undiscovered home talent and these drew forth much social documentation that may not always pass as literature, but that makes the fourteen-year file a quarry of information for the cultural historian. Several young writers who were later to achieve prominence first saw print in this paper. Poems by Patrick Kavanagh appeared. There were extracts from the comic genius of Flann O'Brien. Conor Cruise O'Brien, then still in the Irish civil service, published under the pseudonym of Donat O'Donnell the essays on Catholic writers that were later assembled as *Maria Cross*. Established writers also contributed: Liam O'Flaherty, Frank O'Connor, Elizabeth Bowen, Denis Johnston. Michael Farrell, whose posthumous novel, *Thy Tears Might Cease,* was to make its mark, wrote a regular feature under the pen name Gulliver. One issue was completely devoted to short stories by James Plunkett: it was an unorthodox way of filling up the magazine, and perhaps reflected editorial exhaustion, but the quality of the stories, later collected as *The Trusting and the Maimed,* justified the departure.

Peadar himself contributed three short stories to the earlier issues: "Remembering Kitty," "Why Blame the Seagulls?" and "War." These have not been printed elsewhere. Selections from *The Big Windows,* his last novel, appeared too. But his principal contribution was a series of vigorous commentaries on social, political, and economic problems, usually in an Irish setting, but not infrequently dealing with events abroad, especially if these could be sifted to offer a parallel with Irish problems. As he commented once with reference to O'Faolain's account of his journey in Calabria, he was not particularly interested in this for itself, but he was interested in the light O'Faolain drew from this experience to shed on the problems of Connemara.

The manner in which O'Donnell himself could use well-observed documentation to pinpoint a general social problem is well illustrated in the two articles, "People and Pawnshops" (December 1942) and "Teachers Vote Strike" (November 1945). Both are concerned to show how a relatively small dislocation in the national economy, in these cases arising from strikes, can bear down disproportionately on people already living on the borderline of starvation. The lack of dogmatism is particularly notable since, as a socialist and former trade-union organizer, we should expect O'Donnell to be heavily on the side of the strikers: yet this did not lead him to minimize or whitewash the hardships their actions caused the poor. These articles illustrate, too, the deep compassion and understanding of the lives of the poor that so many witnesses have testified as a trait in Peadar O'Donnell the man.

The same willingness to let the other fellow have his say, while in no way watering down the forceful expression of his own opinions, appears in a discussion of the Northern problem in 1950, which interestingly foreshadows the more violent phase of conflict, which opened twenty years later. O'Donnell's own views on the North reflected the green imperialism of most Republicans: he did not recognize the right of the Northern Protestants to opt out of the island nation. But the vigor of these people had always impressed him, and in *The Bell* for December 1950, he introduced an article he had solicited from the Rev. Frederick Leahy of the National Union of Protestants with the statement:

> The section of our people who intrigue the imagination most today are those who have shut themselves into a rebel statelet in North-east Ulster. They offer as sharp a challenge as the western seaboard in the days of Synge.

Leahy was allowed to have his dig at Catholic tyranny and intolerance in the Republic, and then a southern Protestant, the Rev. Charles Stack of County Limerick, was invited to rebut him. It has traditionally been claimed by Southern republicans of all shades that Protestants under Dublin have no grievances, and it evidently came as a shock to the editor when Stack quietly echoed the charges voiced by Leahy. But he was permitted to have his say, and O'Donnell contributed honestly to the discussion in a fresh editorial, "When a Minority Sulks."

Inevitably the battle over censorship had to be fought over again in the pages of *The Bell,* although it does not appear that the magazine itself ever suffered the attentions of the Irish Censorship Board. In championing the specific demand that any Irish writer be free to speak or write about Irish life in any form he chose, O'Donnell did not confine his strictures to the official censorship. In an editorial, "Liberty Ltd.," he pointed out that even more sinister behind-the-scenes pressures were used to prevent voices the establishment found disturbing from being heard over the radio. When Dr. Noel Browne's attempt to introduce a measure of state medicine was killed by the Catholic hierarchy's pressure on an inter-party government, this provided a further illustration. In a lively editorial, "Suggestion for a Fighting Wake" (June 1947), O'Donnell lamented the failure to establish a Ministry of Fine Arts, as had been foreshadowed during the struggle for independence, and proposed that the best banned book of the year should be ceremoniously waked and buried in traditional Irish fashion in order to satirize the new philistine rulers before the court of world opinion. Soon after this the censorship was eased somewhat by the institution of a system of appeal, and the *Bell's* editor admitted that officialdom was beginning at last to show "glimmerings of adult good sense."

But the principal social-political-economic issue that preoccupied O'Donnell, both inside and outside the

pages of *The Bell,* during these years was the problem
of "saving the West." It is a problem of ancient ancestry, has many ramifications, and has never been settled yet.

The West is the generic term used by both social reformers and tourist-promoters to refer to the small-
farming heartland of the country. Every Irish schoolboy
learns that the wicked Oliver Cromwell gave the native
Irish the alternative of being banished "to Hell or Connaught." Connaught is the province west of the Shannon typified either by mournful wastes of inhospitable
bog or wildernesses of stone, such as the Burren where
one of Cromwell's generals is said to have grumbled
that he found "no tree to hang a man, no earth to bury
a man, not enough water to drown a man." The social
phenomenon of uneconomic smallholdings on which
survivors of the Great Famine struggled to rear large
families extends from O'Donnell's native Donegal in
the north to Kerry and West Cork in the southwest tip
of Munster.

We have seen from the early novels, especially *Islanders* and *Adrigoole,* that the plight of these small
homesteaders, such as his forefathers had been, always
taxed O'Donnell. It was his hope that the "mountainy
men" who mostly took the side of the Republic in the
struggle against the ranchers and property owners of
the midlands and east would profit by the dynamism
of the troubled times to carry through a social revolution and achieve a Workers' and Small Farmers' Republic. Emigration to England and America had been
one particularly distressing feature under British rule.

It was hoped that a native government would reverse this trend and provide employment for her own population within Irish shores. Instead, the rate of emigration increased under the Free State government and continued unabated under de Valera during the interwar years.

When the second world war started, Britain needed men and women for her factories, as well as for her armed forces, and the exodus continued, even though security controls were instituted for travel across the Irish sea. Peadar O'Donnell was anxious to keep in touch with these emigrants and for three years of his life he became a civil servant. He did not particularly want to be burdened with a regular job, but he wished to recover his expenses and he needed official standing to obtain permission to enter wartime Britain. The only way he could secure this was by enrollment as a temporary welfare officer with the Irish Department of Industry and Commerce. Between 1940 and 1943 he crossed frequently to England and Scotland to see conditions for himself. These journeys provided raw materials for several later editorials in *The Bell*. He was favorably impressed by British measures to provide cultural and educational amenities for their troops in isolated billets, and he advocated similar measures to alleviate tedium in isolated Irish countrysides or where sizable groups of displaced workers were collected together in the turf-cutting stations of the midlands. The ending of the war he saw as a crucial challenge for Irish social policy. In an editorial, "Call the Exiles Home" (February 1945), he wrote:

There are a quarter of a million Irish men and women in Britain so recently exiled as to be still on call if signalled to as the war ends. Let the word go out among them, on authority they will trust, that there are jobs to return to at wages on which homes can be rested and they will be back in droves, cheering. But unless the signal is given promptly then these people will make homes for themselves in Britain.

Virtually nothing was done while de Valera remained premier. Some light industries were established during the 1930s behind high tariff protection against the established industrial nations. Lemass, as de Valera's Minister for Industry and Commerce and later successor, passed special legislation to encourage new industries to locate themselves in the West. Afforestation, shamefully neglected during the British occupation, forged steadily ahead. But all this was far from sufficient to check the tide. O'Donnell was tireless in advocating alternatives. He urged cooperatives for tomato-growers, fishermen, beet-farmers, and others, and demanded heavy government loans at low interest to purchase glasshouses, machinery, and workmanlike fishingboats. Other reformers were campaigning on similar lines. Under General Costello's vigorous management the Irish Sugar Company at Tuam in County Galway made firm purchasing contracts and advanced capital for machinery and fertilizers for small farmers who would grow beet for the factory. In Glencolumkille on the Donegal coast, Father McDyer was able to reverse the trend of emigration in one small community through a diversified program of cooperative enterprise. Most of the capital for this, however, came not from government funds, but from Donegal men who had already made good overseas and were prepared to help with money at low interest rates. Other small ventures came into being, such as the Connemara Fishermen's Co-operative, embracing virtually all the lobsterfishermen of the coast, the Irish Co-operative Development Trust, and the Gleninagh Sheepfarmer's Co-operative. But their total contribution was small in relation to the size of the problem.

The whole issue of the decline of the West is a complex one. From 1948 to 1954 a government commission, of which O'Donnell was a member, studied the problem and eventually published a massive volume: *Report of the Commission on Emigration and other Population Problems.* The majority of the commission stressed subjective factors in causing emigration: Peadar believed this was secondary and entered a dissenting opinion in which he insisted that the situation arose directly from "the scarcity of reasonably secure employment for men." He believed that a remedy must involve not simply wide-scale relief works, but a massive expansion of the whole national economy. A decade later, in a pamphlet "The Role of the Industrial Workers in the Problems of the West," he seems to concede that the forefront of the problem is the *frustration* of life in the small farming communities, but he still believed that it was through direct economic measures that this could be remedied.

After *The Bell* ceased publication in 1954, Peadar continued active in a variety of interlocking committees and campaigns, both in Ireland and abroad. Already before the war he had visited Germany to preside over the opening session of the European Small Farmers' Conference held in Berlin in 1930. In later years he visited Finland, Poland, Hungary, Czechoslovakia, and Rumania as Irish delegate to various peace congresses. He never visited Russia. What impressed him most in these international assemblies was the similarity in outlook between peasant smallholders throughout the world. Returning to Ireland after one such session, he told a friend that while listening to a conversation in halting English with a Croatian and a Chinese peasant, he suddenly had a feeling that he was in the presence of "my uncle Johnnie with his shoulder against the door, and he looking out across the fields."

In the 1950s O'Donnell was a member of the World Peace Council, and he visited Belfast several times in connection with a body eventually called "The Provisional Committee for the Abolition of the Atom Bomb." A Northern correspondent stresses Peadar's success as chairman in getting Protestants, Catholics, Republicans, Communists, and Quakers to work together. When the Vietnam war developed, Peadar O'Donnell and Dan Breen, another veteran of the Irish struggle, felt that as the oldest of the anti-imperialist nations, Ireland should make her views known. A small body called the "Irish Voice on Vietnam" was the result. In the 1960s Saturday mornings in the O'Donnell home in Drumcondra became a forum for general discussion in a new "Save the West" campaign. A thoughtful English journalist, Michael Viney, and his Mayo-born wife, Eithne, provided useful publicity. Subsequently the movement snowballed. Public meetings at which bishops (strange shades of the past!) appeared on the platform were held in Galway, Charlestown, Foxford, and other centers. They drew large audiences and got good press coverage. The National Farmers' Association joined in the agitation, and the government even set up a Council for the West. Practical measures, however, were lacking, and the movement withered gently away.

Looked at in objective retrospect, Peadar O'Donnell's life as a publicist might seem—as he ruefully suggested in an interview in 1972—a campaign for lost causes. The Republicans lost in the civil war. Later attempts to give the cause a social context and spur on to victory proved fruitless. The agitation over the Land Annuities was taken over by the constitutionalists and blunted by compromise. The long struggle to save the West seems to have ended in defeat. Yet history may hesitate to endorse a purely negative verdict. In 1970, for the first time in nearly a century, the population figures for the Twenty-six Counties of the Irish Republic showed an upward trend. Economists recorded other hopeful signs: the marriage rate was increasing, and the age at marriage, once the highest in Europe, coming down. One cannot tell what repercussions the political events of the early 1970s may have, but perhaps posterity will note that a turning-point in Ireland's social development was passed at this point. If so, O'Donnell's persistent, sanguine, sometimes flamboyantly conducted campaigns of the thirties, forties, fifties, and sixties of this century may seem a not insignificant factor in this development.

9

The Big Windows

There is an interval of twenty-one years between the
publication of *On the Edge of the Stream*, the last of
O'Donnell's early novels, and that of *The Big Windows*,
which appeared in 1954. As with so much of his life
and work, the seed from which this novel sprang was
sown during the fighting of the troubled times. After
he had been wounded by the British, but escaped capture, he lay convalescing on a bed of straw in a friendly
farmhouse in a remote glen of Donegal. It was then
that he noticed something unusual in the bond between
the young woman of the house and her mother-in-law.
Often in rural Ireland this relationship is distinguished
by an almost cannibal rivalry, but these two could
laugh together like older and younger sister. The seed
ripened slowly over the years until *The Big Windows*
became the most complex of all Peadar's books. Into
it he put a lifetime's observation of country ways of
feeling coupled with the mellow compassion that always
distinguished him.

Superficially the book's theme is simple. Tom Manus, a vigorous small farmer from a backward glen in Donegal, marries an island woman and one evening brings her home. But this incident and its aftermath are the pretext for a portrayal in depth of life in this small, self-contained community. The townland, disturbed by the event, is a living entity:

> Who knows how a townland at odds with itself over some sudden departure from pattern, strives to find its way back to peace; if a townland cannot have peace it cannot survive. It whispers to itself, recounts its experiences, measures itself against this new reality and thus promotes its own growth, disowns, discards, accepts, while all the time it is uneasy and easily roused to noise. It was a little thing that a man should go out of view to find himself a wife and they could easily have accommodated her within their pattern. It was a widening of the world but it was not altogether new. The thing was, the glen had not made itself ready. Nobody pictured them arriving in the dark. Nobody foresaw that Susan (who once had a feeling for Tom) would go back in on herself, and somehow rouse in the glen its old, old dislike for strangers.

Events in the foreground of the story are told against the rigid background of community life, which is dictated by the need to be neighborly and the need to survive, which sometimes conflict. "It is right to be good-neighbourly. It is wrong to be soft. A man needs to have a good greed for the world in him," Mary Manus early advises her daughter-in-law. Sometimes the issue is put in more general terms: "There is a great wrestling match between the world and the people in it," another character observes. Elsewhere this peasant shrewdness appears in its earthiest terms, as when the physical qualities of the new wife are studied and discussed as if she represented a new strain in cattle:

> Turn round let you. A fine frame of a woman, Mary; no fat on her rump. She is nature's own woman, Mary, for, like I often said, no matter what it is rears its young from milk if the fat is on the rump it will not be where it should be. . . . She is the right strain of a woman for this glen. She is light in the bone. I'm saying all the time that this glen needs a lighter strain than is in it. People are getting too bulky. Too much bone. It is the lime, Mary, that's what I say.

Behind this, too, is the author's own mature judgment of people and character, which he puts into the mouth of the wiser characters in the book. Here is Aunt Peggy on Brigid's mother-in-law:

> Mary is a great woman Brigid. She is a woman life beat hard, and it bent her a wee bit, like you see, for she carried a heavy burden, but ever and always there was the calm in her you see now; and the sense. There is something else in her too Brigid: holiness I think.

Mary is a dour character and it was a common saying among the neighbors that it would go hard with the young wife that came in on her floor. To everyone's surprise she and the islandwoman hit it off from the word go, and not by the younger woman's making all the concessions either.

Gaiety, harshness, lively humor, and grim tragedy alternate in the book's course, like cloud shadows flitting across April fields—the obscene jeering of the neighbor women at Brigid's arrival in the village, the symbolic breaking out of the big windows in the mountain-dark cottage, the fisherman's net to keep the hens out of the oats, which is the wonder of the village, Ann the Hill's strangeness, the killing of the dog that was worrying sheep, the christening to mark Brigid's acceptance in the glen, the drunken home-coming after the first days out selling lime.

In the earlier books, as already noted, O'Donnell's style is plain and direct. Here it is an artefact, just as Synge's or Lady Gregory's was. It still draws its strength from a realistic vision of country life, but it has now a slow, reflective rhythm, particularly in the passages that point a moral, which perfectly suits the author's mature purpose. Here is an example. Aunt Peggy has told the story of a fight in the glen a generation ago, subtly warning of the danger of a similar fight breaking out now between Dan Rua and Tom Manus over their wives' feuding. The story does not fall on deaf ears:

Susan (Dan Rua's wife) made for home, half running. The glen watched her race over the fields. They saw Dan Rua stand like a man in a daze, and then turn and look after Susan, start across the fields with long, strong strides, and go inside and shut the door behind him, and it was a great wonder to them, and they ran out from their doorways calling to one another and there was no laughter in any of them. They kept their eye on that shut door, and nobody dared to send children to listen. And then the door opened and Dan Rua stepped forth, his pipe was in his mouth, and in the calm they could see the puffs of smoke rising; it was as if he was cheering. He picked up a shovel and sauntered over to Tom Manus, and he took the hammer from Tom's hand and he struck blows that were heard half the length of the glen, helping Tom put in the big windows.

The Big Windows is O'Donnell's epitaph on a way of life whose actual character and whose social context he understood better than any writer of his generation. Yet he does not here bemoan its passing, as perhaps he did in *Adrigoole*. For him the Big Windows were always opening on a new world, different, but just as good as the old. The Ireland of the cloistered glen, which had its grandeurs and its miseries, has passed. The Big Windows are in, and we can look out at the world and the world can look in on us. What shall we make of each other?

Bibliography

NOVELS

Storm. Dublin: The Talbot Press. n.d. (1925)
Islanders. London: Jonathan Cape, 1928. New York: G. P. Putnam's, 1928. American edition entitled *The Way it Was with Them.*
Adrigoole. London: Cape, 1929. New York: Putnam's, 1929.
The Knife. London: Cape, 1930. New York: Putnam's, 1931, as *There Will be Fighting.*
On the Edge of the Stream. London: Cape, 1934.
The Big Windows. London: Cape, 1955.

AUTOBIOGRAPHY

The Gates Flew Open. London: Cape, 1932.
Salud! An Irishman in Spain. London: Methuen, 1937.
There Will be Another Day. Dublin: Dolmen Press, 1963.

DRAMA

Wrack. London: Cape, 1933.

PAMPHLETS

For or Against the Ranchers? Irish Working Farmers in the Economic War. Westport: Mayo News, 1932.

The Bothy Fire and All That. With reprint of article on Arranmore Disaster. Dublin: Irish Press, 1937.

The Problem of the West. Swinford: Mayo Magazine, 1966. reprinted as *The Role of the Industrial Workers in the Problem of the West* by Docas Co-operative Society, Dublin. n.d.

SHORT STORIES

"Remembering Kitty." *The Bell* 1, no. 1. (Dublin monthly periodical, 1940–1954).

"Why Blame the Seagulls?" *The Bell* 1, no. 3.

"War." *The Bell* 15, no. 3.

ARTICLES AND EDITORIALS IN *The Bell*

"Comment on the Foregoing 2, no. 3.

"The Dumb Multitudinous Masses." 2, no. 4.

"Migration is a Way of Keeping Grip." 3, no. 2.

"Belfast—Village or Capital?" 4, no. 6.

"People and Pawnshops." 5, no. 3.

"Cry Jew!" 5, no. 6.

"The Irish in Britain." 6, no. 7.

"Call the Exiles Home." 9, no. 5.

"Teachers Vote Strike." 11, no. 2.

"Work in Progress." 11, no. 3.

   (Comprises opening sections of *The Big Windows.*)

"Signing On." 12, no. 1.

"At the Sign of the Donkey-cart." 12, no. 2.

"The Myth of Irish Fascism." 12, no. 3.

"Liberty Ltd." 12, no. 4.

"Grandchildren of the Insurrection." 12, no. 5.

"Under the Writer's Torch." 12, no. 6.

"Facts and Fairies." 13, no. 1.

"A Word from Wexford." 13, no. 2.

"A Word to Young Writers." 13, no. 4.

" (i) Whose Bridgehead? (ii) Exiles." 13, no. 5.

"Palestine." 13, no. 6.

"Portrait of the Parish." 14, no. 1.

"Palestine." 14, no. 2.

"Suggestion for a Fighting Wake." 14, no. 4.

"Tourists' Guide to Irish Politics." 14, no. 5.

"An Unfinished Study." 14, no. 6.

"Our Mythical Fascism Again." 15, no. 1.

"Somewhat Displaced Persons." 15, no. 2.

"Publishing in Ireland." 15, no. 4.

"Ghosts." 15, no. 5.

"National Theatre." 15, no. 6.

"A Recognisable Gait of Going" and "Dead Houses in Connacht." 16, no. 2.

"A Welcome to a Contributor." 16, no. 3.

"When a Minority Sulks." 16, no. 4.

"Pointer to an Article." 16, no. 6.

"The Principle at Issue." 17, no. 2.

"Opening a Discussion." 17, no. 6.

"De Valera's Speech on Emigration." 17, no. 7.

"Taking Stock." 18, no. 8.

"And Again, Publishing in Ireland." 18, no. 10.

"The Irish Press and O Faolain." 18, no. 11.

"World Peace Congress." 18, no. 12.

"An Announcement—A Request" and "The Orangeman." 19, no. 1.

"Up Stormont Way." 19, no. 2.

"A Pilgrim has been Among Us." 19, no. 3.

"Changing the Content." 19, no. 4.

"East-West Trade and its Bearing on the Gaeltacht." 19, no. 10.

SECONDARY MATERIAL

Bell, J. Bowyer. *The Secret Army.* (London: Anthony Blond, 1970).

Gilmore, George. *The Republican Congress 1934.* (Dublin: Dochas Co-op. Society, n.d.) c. 1970.

Greaves, C. Desmond. *Liam Mellows and the Irish Revolution.* (London: Lawrence & Wishart, 1971).

Macardle, Dorothy. *The Irish Republic.* (London: Gollancz, 1938).

Manning, Maurice. *The Blueshirts.* (Dublin: Gill and Macmillan, 1970).

McInerney, Michael. *Peadar O'Donnell—Ulster Socialist Republican.* (in preparation) (This is an expansion of a series of articles appearing in *The Irish Times,* 1968). Dublin: E. & T. O'Brien.

Reports of the Commission on Emigration and other Population Problems 1948–1954 (Dublin, Stationery Office). O'Donnell was a member of this Commission and recorded a dissenting opinion.